Broadcasting and Youth

A study commissioned by
the British Broadcasting Corporation,
the Calouste Gulbenkian Foundation,
the Independent Broadcasting Authority
and the Manpower Services Commission.

Published by the Calouste Gulbenkian Foundation
UK and Commonwealth Branch, London.
1979

Printed by Oyez Press, London

ISBN 0-903319-14-4

Contents

Chairman's Introduction

This Study was commissioned by the Calouste Gulbenkian Foundation and the Manpower Services Commission (MSC) in association with the Independent Broadcasting Authority and the British Broadcasting Corporation. It developed out of initiatives taken separately and earlier by the BBC and the IBA's Education Departments. These in turn were a response to the MSC's Report *Young People and Work* which concentrated on the difficulties of young people facing unemployment or work of an unsatisfying and perhaps intermittent nature.

Stimulated by the *Holland Report*, as *Young People and Work* is commonly called, the broadcasters wondered if, within the proposed strategy for countering the impact of long term unemployment, there might be a contribution which educational broadcasting could make. Simultaneously but separately, the broadcasting organisations concluded that the topic should not be limited to the young unemployed. It should cover also, and perhaps especially, those least able to face the more severe consequences of transition from school to work. Additionally, the broadcasters realised that to limit the debate to the impact of designated educational broadcasting would be artificial and restricting. Even more significantly, they were agreed that the needs of the young people should transcend the individual interests of the IBA and the Independent Companies and the BBC. On this basis they approached the MSC and the Calouste Gulbenkian Foundation, both deeply involved already in the problems of young people.

After consultation with a working party under my chairmanship, it was decided to establish a short project to be known as the Young Adult Study, with terms of reference outlined on page 4, under the guidance of a Steering Committee whose membership is listed on page 6. The Study has been financed by the Manpower

1

Services Commission and the Gulbenkian Foundation. On their side the IBA and the BBC contributed by the secondment of Jean Sargeant and Neil Barnes respectively, both senior education officers within their organisations, to act as Project Officers on a full-time basis for six months. David Moore, Principal of Nelson and Colne College, was then invited to become part-time Director of the Study. Janis Tilbrook was Project Administrator initially, and was succeeded by Stevie Dixon who was largely responsible for collating material relating to the present broadcast provision. Arthur Bowley and Ray Brown were also appointed on a part-time basis as researchers. Arthur Bowley's work provided the Project Officers with demographic background to their enquiries. The analysis of the relationship between young adults and the media largely reflects the valuable work of Ray Brown. Industrial Facts and Forecasting Ltd (IFF), the organisation responsible for much of the background research to the *Holland Report*, interviewed selected employers and young people in groups and individually. Jean Sargeant and Neil Barnes, as full-time Project Officers, talked to broadcasters and representatives of a wide range of organisations concerned with young people.

Appendix IV lists the principal contacts made by the Project Officers. Many other less official contacts and consultations also enriched our Study. The first thanks of the four Sponsors, therefore, must go to the many individuals and organisations in many parts of the UK who gave their time, experience and advice to guide our work and help formulate our recommendations. In the same context we thank also our Steering Committee who contributed individually and collectively to periodic assessment of the Study's development at meetings which were always vigorous and controversial. Finally, but not least, we thank the Project Team and their assistants. They worked all hours under intense pressure and far beyond what had been planned or could be expected, even knowing the commitment with which they approached the task.

Given the short-term, limited nature of the exercise, and notwithstanding some previously held knowledge and experience, we realised from the beginning that the Study would pose as many questions as it would produce recommendations. We do not think that this is a weakness provided early action is taken to answer the questions. Some of the answers may need to take the form of further enquiries or studies which could be more significant than anything attempted here. Others will be practical schemes of one sort or another.

Considerations of this kind guided the final structure of the Report. Informal in style, it begins like *Young People and Work*, with a brief summary of the main argument. Immediately following is a description of the needs of young people and their use of the media including, of course, a summary of the present approach of the broadcasters to young people. The Report concludes with the recommendations we think necessary if the needs of young people are to be met adequately. Some of the recommendations require additional resources but principally they require changes of approach and attitude. We hope that the arguments we present are persuasive enough to effect these changes as rapidly as possible. In particular we have urged that the momentum of the Study be developed through a small, permanent coordinating unit — a Young Adult Unit perhaps — in which young people themselves will play a part and which will facilitate the capacity of broadcasters and related agencies to meet young adult needs.

To achieve this end a quite new degree of cooperation will be necessary. Hence one of the keynotes of the Report is the value of cooperation. But cooperation is not just a matter for broadcasters and related agencies. It must include also other media and involve, especially, cooperation between the providers and the receivers, broadcasters and young adults. Hence the importance of the Young Adult Unit. Such cooperation can arise only from adequate information stimulating a mutual understanding. The Calouste Gulbenkian Foundation publishes this Report as a first contribution towards such understanding and in the hope that its findings will be used by all concerned as a basis for immediate discussion leading to immediate action.

Peter Brinson

Young Adult Study

Terms of reference

1. To determine the contribution of broadcasting — in association with other agencies and educational methods — to help

   i   educate and train young adults of all kinds, particularly the unemployed and disadvantaged, whether or not they are already undertaking any kind of education or training, so that they may gain a wider, more informed understanding of the problems and opportunities associated with all aspects of work — or the lack of it — including, where appropriate, basic vocational and non-vocational skills;

   ii   other groups of adults concerned with the development and well-being of the young people above, such as parents, teachers, lecturers, managers, counsellors, etc.

2. Specifically to

   i   gather information about the existing total provision (broadcast and otherwise) for the people described above;

   ii   pick out target groups and comment on the sorts of provision required by them;

   iii advise on the subject areas and arrangements which, within the total campaign, might be treated in a sequential and structured way, combining broadcasting with print, face-to-face tuition, etc;

   iv investigate suitable hours for the broadcast provision;

   v   suggest alternative operational models for reasonable

4

broadcast and non-broadcast contributions to the campaign together with estimates of associated costs, where appropriate;

vi   suggest possible plans of implementation and time-scales indicating the degree of urgency of parts of the plan of campaign;

vii   judge how much and what kind of support there would be (and would need to be) for a campaign based on broadcasting amongst interested parties, including target groups, the Department of Education and Science, MSC, local authorities, further education colleges, employers, trade unions, voluntary organisations and the like;

viii   make any other relevant comments.

Young Adult Study

Members of Steering Committee

Peter Brinson (Chairman)	Director, UK & Commonwealth Branch, Calouste Gulbenkian Foundation
Robert Aitken	Director of Education, Coventry
Martin Baker	Assistant Secretary, Higher and Further Education, Department of Education and Science
Squire Barraclough	Chief Information Officer, Confederation of British Industries
John Cain	Assistant Controller of Educational Broadcasts, BBC
Richard Freeman	Executive Director, National Extension College
Richard Hoggart	Warden, Goldsmiths' College Chairman, Advisory Council for Adult and Continuing Education
Geoffrey Holland	Director of Special Programmes, Manpower Services Commission
Jeremy Isaacs	At outset of Study was Director of Programmes, Thames Television
Roy Jackson	Secretary, Education Committee, Trades Union Congress

Young Adult Study: Members of Steering Committee

Geoffrey Melling	Director, Further Education Curriculum Review and Development Unit
David Moore	Principal, Nelson and Colne College
John Robinson	Education Secretary, BBC
Kim Taylor	Head of Education Programme Services, IBA

The argument

1. In the UK and throughout the western world a rapidly growing proportion of young people appears to be faced with the almost certain prospect of periods of prolonged unemployment brought about by fundamental changes in the structure of industry and commerce. However, many young people currently in employment find that a lack of initial basic educational skills, together with the lack of access to training facilities at work, means that their ability to adapt to these changes is also very restricted.

2. Concern is felt, in this country, that unemployment is being disproportionately borne by the younger age groups who, without experience of work, have only recently arrived on a stagnant job market. Moreover, this burden falls most heavily on those who are already disadvantaged in other respects by race or sex prejudice, family background and mental or physical handicap. Much worse, the very success of our educational system in upgrading the qualifications of more young people has made the deficiencies of that 20% who leave school without them so much more prominent. This development has occurred within the last 15 years and it is perhaps surprising that we have not so far considered its consequences, which include making this group more vulnerable to unemployment.

3. Many people leave school with a feeling of failure or rejection and face the possibility of unemployment and other consequences of rapidly changing economic and social conditions. They are likely to have rejected formal education and any systems of support which appear to share the characteristics of school. Consequently, it is unlikely that they will be well disposed to receiving advice from official sources or having to learn skills they have already failed to master by traditional methods; their very

failure will make them equally suspicious of exhortations and inducements to learn new skills. It therefore becomes very important for those who wish to help and support this group to consider the widest possible means not only of compensating for inadequate basic education, but also opening up a new range of survival skills by using the most effective methods, however untraditional they may be.

4. Apart from the need to manage the transfer from the mostly supportive ethos of home and school to the relatively laissez-faire world of work and legal independence, these young people also face the physical and emotional problems of late adolescence. Evidence suggests that here, too, the needs are not being adequately met by the existing agencies.

5. And it is not just the young people themselves who are short of information and advice; their teachers, careers guidance staff, employers, their older fellow-workers and, above all their parents, are also often uncertain how best to help.

6. The broadcasting media have demonstrated how uniquely effective they are in reaching, influencing and stimulating large sections of the population including those not normally receptive to the academic approach. But more than this, when working in collaboration with other agencies they have been seen to play a crucial role in developing and delivering new and attractive forms of information, advice-giving and educational experience.

7. Broadcasting to schools and colleges is a well-tried and effective means of reaching some sections of young people via their teachers; this form of broadcasting is clearly restricted in terms of scheduling, content and, some would argue, style. There are, however, no other departments or sections within the broadcasting organisations which are specifically concerned with producing programmes for teenagers or young adults, and this may also have contributed to the failure to develop the full potential of general broadcasting. Certainly young people are rarely specifically catered for.

8. The successful use of phone-in programmes and other forms of advice and counselling on the air, and the extended use of broadcasts as integrated parts of informational or educational projects in the community nationally or locally, point the way to the use

of broadcasting as an effective means of reaching and motivating young people and their parents. Recent experience suggests that such developments can take place without compromising the creative independence of the broadcasters or the professional skills of collaborating organisations. However, such extended activity (*eg* referral services, counselling, study groups, provision of information) of which the broadcast may only be the first step, falls outside the broadcasters' specific remit and expertise, and requires a constancy of provision not normally expected of broadcast output.

9. In the light of the seriousness of the problems facing many young people, the broadcasting organisations should *acknowledge* the key social role which they are able to play, *review* their current policies regarding programming for young people and *encourage* the production of appropriate new programmes as well as fostering the development of existing ones. Most importantly, they should *co-operate* with relevant agencies, particularly, though not exclusively, in relation to the MSC's Youth Opportunities Programme (YOP), in setting up machinery to ensure that contacts initially made via broadcasting can be taken up and developed.

10. Some collaborative ventures are, of course, already taking place and we would certainly hope that this trend will continue. However, we believe that this development might be fostered by setting up a small unit which would not only illuminate young people's needs and initiate collaborative ventures, but also provide and store information, make introductions, evaluate and co-ordinate the efforts of those seeking to alleviate — through recommended use of the media — the difficulties of those young people at risk.

Part I

The Context

1 Who are we talking about and why?

1.0 Part I of this Report looks at those groups of young people most in need of help and advice during their transition from school to work; the needs which they say they have and are said by others to have, and what is known about their use of and reaction to the mass media. This Chapter is concerned with identifying those groups of young people most in need.

1.1 Although the main concern of this Study is the transition from school to work, it is of course impossible to pursue this concern in separation from the overall situation of young people as they move from dependent childhood to more or less independent adulthood. One of our informants, Pat White, Principal Careers Officer for the Inner London Education Authority (ILEA) commented that we expect a lot from young people leaving school. At the very age at which they are experiencing the greatest personal changes — physiologically, psychologically and socially — we expect them, without the benefit of experience, to be able to make sensible choices not only about employment but also about marriage and a host of other long term commitments. It may be worth reminding ourselves of the range of events and processes which are involved in this transition from school to adult life. During less than a ten year period most young people

— cease compulsory education
— cease emotional dependence on parents and teachers
— cease financial dependence on parents
— acquire political and legal independence
— make critical career choices
— make a transfer to employment with all its implications for change of life style
— face, in some cases, the prospect of unemployment, perhaps

without any experience of employment
— endure categorisation by examination successes or failures
— assume the responsibility for a home
— experience the final years of physical development and growth.

1.2 Just to make matters more complex, even in the one field of education and training, the array of options at 16+ is growing in number and degree. For example, staying on in full-time education may mean a traditional selective sixth form, a comprehensive sixth form, a sixth form college, a college of further education or a tertiary college. If the choice is to leave school, then the young person may be faced with employment which leads to a career and encourages further education and training, or dead-end work where further education is positively discouraged. Much worse, there is the possibility of being faced with no employment at all.

1.3 The wonder perhaps is that so many young people emerge relatively unscathed from the process. But it must be said that in the context of this country's current economic and social problems, particularly in relation to the high levels of youth unemployment, the hazards faced by some young people are greatly increased and the numbers still unharmed at the end are likely to be fewer. Moreover, all these aspects of the period of transition should perhaps be set against one general 'disadvantage', that is, that they have been in, and may only now be slowly emerging from a position of subordination.

1.4 This notion of subordination should be seen in relation to their parents, to their teachers and, very likely, in the work place too. At home, at school and at work they tend not be be masters of their destinies, nor to be able easily to discover how to proceed along the road to greater independence and self-realisation. They are 'handicapped' by a background of emotional dependence on their family, a lack of experience of the world outside the home and school and, for many, a shortage of money. Room for manoeuvre is often limited and independence frequently has to be struggled for. The world of work offers the chance of this independence. For some it presents the opportunities for a wider range of social contacts; for others, the fulfilment of individual talents or skills; and for all, through the regular provision of an income, the chance to participate in the various elements of today's youth culture. If this period of young adulthood is, as it is generally regarded, to be a period of personal and social experimentation, and if the nature of the world we live in changes with ever increasing rapidity, it is safe to predict that it would be impossible to offer too great a provision of disinterested advice and counselling about how to cope with the world — emotionally, socially, at work and at leisure.

1.5 Not all these aspects of 'transition' relate directly to our terms of reference, but it is important to see them as a backcloth to the work-orientated aspects of this Study. Indeed, when one focuses on the world of work and preparation for it, the increased emphasis on qualifications and training, the decline of traditional industries and the development of new ones, the changing perceptions of the roles of women in relation to employment, one cannot but believe that all these, coupled with the effect of rising levels of unemployment, must present a confusing picture to many young adults and, indeed, to their parents.

1.6 This Report is too short to allow for an examination of the area of transition from school to adult life in any great detail, but supporting material and evidence may be found in a variety of national and international publications.[1] This material and other evidence from various sources illustrates the general problem of transition from school to work. It also highlights the more severe difficulty of those young people, who for one reason or another, are most likely to have to bear the brunt of what many in Western industrial societies now accept as inevitable structural unemployment. It is becoming apparent also that a predictable group of young people will carry this burden of permanent or intermittent unemployment, or of work which lacks any sort of satisfaction or status.

Such young people are likely to include those more obviously disadvantaged by race, colour or sex prejudice, family background, physical or mental handicap. In addition, evidence from such

---

1 The following may be of particular interest: *From Education to Working Life* — EEC (12/76); *Youth Employment* — EEC (4/77); *Youth Education Employment* — Institute of Education of the European Cultural Foundation; *Entry of Young People into Working Life* and *Beyond Compulsory Schools* — both OECD (1977 and 1976 respectively); more locally, *Variety or Chaos* — Association of College Principals, (1978), expresses a different dimension of the problems.

sources as the House of Commons Select Committee on *The Attainment of the School Leaver* suggests that another minority is beginning to emerge. This new minority is identified by its lack of any kind of academic accreditation or certification. As recently as fifteen years ago only a minority of school leavers had any qualifications. Now the position is completely reversed. Only 17% leave school with no qualifications, but these non-achievers are more obviously exposed to the stigma of public failure.

1.7 We believe that in considering the needs of young adults in relation to the world of work it is useful to have an outline structure into which detailed needs can be fitted. One such structure we have found useful as a working model is provided by David Ashton and David Field in their recent book *Young Workers*. We summarise it here as a starting point for subsequent analysis and discussion.

1.8 Ashton and Field divide young people into three broad occupational groups: the *careerless*, those in *short term career* jobs and those in *extended careers*. The first of the three are those who enter semi-skilled or unskilled work. The second group enter middle streams of the school system and take up, or try to take up, skilled manual and lower grade technical or clerical work. The final group are those who are in the higher streams of the school system and enter similar jobs to their middle class parents. Using 1966 sample census data, they estimate that the proportions of these groups throughout the *whole* of the working population were 30%, 50% and 17% respectively.

1.9 The group of schoolchildren 'destined' to join the *careerless* category, and to do so without experiencing serious problems of adjustment, have in common a general alienation from the ethos of school and its academic studies. They see themselves and are perceived as being no good at school work, but do not regard themselves as failures. So the acquisition of an unskilled or semi-skilled job is something to look forward to, providing a welcome change from school and giving them the monetary means to improve their lifestyle. They seek gratification in the here and now. The job is looked on as a means of making money and making friends; it is not regarded itself as a source of fulfilment. Fulfilment comes from participation in the dominant youth culture and this absorbs a large proportion of their time and money.

1.10 The second group, those heading for *short term* (or limited) *careers* and who will make an easy adjustment, will have had a moderately successful school life. They recognise the importance of the school-based values of doing well, though this is seen in practical terms of the improvement of future job opportunities. They reject the idea of unskilled or semi-skilled work as being 'dead-end jobs' and seek instead an occupation where they can 'make something of themselves'. Immediate gratification in the form of high wages is rejected in favour of future prospects and the opportunity of further education or training. Their work is one source of fulfilment to them. Their reliance on the dominant youth culture as a source of support is less than for the *careerless*.

1.11 The third group, those who go for *extended careers*, although drawn predominantly from children of middle class parents also includes a sizeable number from the working class. The group includes those who leave school with GCE qualifications and go directly into managerial, administrative and commercial occupations, and those who take some form of full-time higher education. This group fully shares the ethos of the 'academic' school and its value systems. The job is seen as providing a large measure of satisfaction and self-identity.

1.12 In each of these categories Ashton and Field stress that for the majority of children the ethos of home has a very important influence on the child in determining the pattern of school life. The response of school teachers and the school system to the child reinforces this and leads to a self-defining range of job choices being perceived as natural, appropriate and satisfying by the child, teacher and parent. In times of full employment and a range of job choices, these children by and large are able to make the transition from school to work without too much difficulty, though not necessarily as easily as they might.

1.13 But Ashton and Field indicate a number of groups who face particular problems in making the move into work. Taking the *careerless* as a group, they point out how remote their attitudes to work are from those who might provide them with help and guidance, except for their parents and friends. The prevailing

17

ethos of the school and of the careers service and of those who work there, tend to run counter to their own —

> "We should stress that the deficiencies do not stem simply from a lack of knowledge on the part of teachers. What is needed is not simply more information about 'careerless' work on the part of teachers but also an appreciation that the values which have guided them in their own careers are inappropriate for young people who wish to enter semi-skilled or unskilled work . . ."

The careers service, too, they feel is at fault for not appreciating what *careerless* young people see as important differences between jobs —

> "If Careers Officers are to gain their respect and co-operation they must have a realistic appreciation of the young people's distinctive view of the world. Unless they acquire this their effectiveness will be greatly hindered, for the young people become critical and distrustful of the agencies when they offer what is seen as unrealistic advice based on a lack of understanding of their problems and a refusal to listen to them."

Neither do their eventual employers usually provide any form of real induction schemes or extended training. They don't need to, since on the whole such employees are easy to find. But for those newly out of school the transition to work is made all the more abrupt as a result. The authors believe that, as a result, one half of all young men and a minority of women in the *careerless* category experience serious problems at this transitional stage. And this is the category which has least sympathy with outside support agencies.

1.14 But there is a group *within* this *careerless* category which is in an even more disadvantaged position — those with a careerless perspective and who are unable to find any job. These are the bottom of the heap.

> "From their point of view they have 'failed' again; this time to find the work that would enable them to maintain their longed for independence. Even those who at school were also treated as having similarly limited abilities now appear to have some qualities that these unemployed people do not have."

Without a job they have less money to participate in those

leisure activities which contribute most to giving them a sense of identity. Within this group of the unemployed Ashton and Field single out the most disadvantaged group of them all, the children and grandchildren of immigrant minority groups having perhaps in addition to all the other difficulties listed, those of discrimination, poor command of English and conflict between their home background and that of the world of work.

1.15 But the disadvantaged and those experiencing difficulty at this transitional stage are to be found elsewhere than among the *careerless*. The authors distinguish one major group to be found among their two 'career-minded' categories. These are the young people who fail to achieve the sort of jobs that they, their parents and their schools thought were appropriate to them. They may fail to do so either because the job opportunities in their area do not exist, or because they have not achieved sufficiently good examination results, or because dissatisfaction with initial job choices has led them to leave their employment. Whatever the cause, the effect is likely to be deep feeling of personal failure and inadequacy, and tension in their relationships in the family. One result may be that they try to get more qualifications at, say, a college of further education. But if by eighteen or nineteen the matter hasn't been resolved, the system provides little support. In any event, the authors feel that Careers Officers are unable, if only because of their heavy case loads, to establish with such people the appropriately close relationships necessary to provide adequate support and guidance.

1.16 These particular categories of need identified by Ashton and Field also emerged, to a large extent, in the course of the Study's investigations. And while in this Report we are concerned with *all* young adults, we concentrate on those groups highlighted above. First, those with minimal school leaving skills for whom the statutory agencies are least well able to provide guidance. Secondly, those within this group who experience long spells of unemployment, and thirdly, those at whatever level of academic or vocational training for whom the expected and appropriate sort of job, or indeed perhaps any job at all, has eluded them.

1.17 It is important to note that in terms of raw numbers, there-fore, we are talking about a very large number of young people indeed. In 1976, in the UK, there were about 5¾ million young people between the ages of fourteen and twenty-one. About 2¼ million of them were in full-time education in school, and another million on full or part-time courses in other educational institutions, particularly colleges of further education. That leaves approximately 2½ million with no formal contact with educational institutions of any kind. It is within this group, the underqualified and those in jobs with minimum security, that unemployment is most frequently experienced.

These young people may, however, have many problems in common with their more advantaged peers. Youth unemployment is, indeed, currently running at about 12% (though with very much higher rates in certain regions or cities), but the prevailing economic climate puts pressures on young people, employed and unemployed alike. Thus, it seems to us, particularly given job mobility (9 million workers change jobs every year), that *all* young people need more and better help, information, advice and support if they are to make a smooth transition from the dependence of school to the independence of adult life.

2   Who needs what?

2.0 The previous Chapter examined categories of young people who more than others were at this time in particular need of help, information and advice in the process of facing the realities of the world of work in particular, and adulthood in general. In this Chapter we look in some detail at what those whom we consulted felt to be the major areas of need, not only for young adults themselves, but also for those people who, as parents, teachers, careers officers, youth workers, employers, have responsibility for them.

2.1 The young people consulted during the course of the Study gave us their views about their own needs. The professional workers, providing agencies and employers had views not only about their own professional needs, but also about the needs of young people themselves during the period of transition from school to the responsibilities of adult life. Perhaps surprisingly, adults and young people alike pointed to the same broad areas. Many adults emphasised that the needs existing during the period of transition were common to most young people, not just the disadvantaged, and that these needs were far from new.

2.2 The needs of young people

2.2.1 Unemployment

There was general and considerable concern over the recent tendency for a limited section of young people, normally the less academically qualified, to be expected to bear the burden of structural unemployment. There was particular dismay over the fact that those most at risk are the *careerless* young people who, frequently alienated from the school system, were particularly looking forward to the real or imagined benefits of employment as a recognition of their dignity as individuals, but who, because of the absence of jobs, were then denied even the minor triumph of being paid for their services, however routine and mundane. Thus, in addition to the help that young people themselves felt they needed in order to face the future, in both psychological and practical ways, professionals and employers felt there was a need to explain not only the underlying social causes of unemployment but to point out that unemployment was not necessarily a reflection of a young person's worth.

Unemployment is demoralising enough for those young people whose backgrounds have given them every reason to feel personally secure and confident. Those who, for example, are black or have come from backgrounds which are disadvantaged in one or multiple ways, may find themselves simply unable to cope and may, many fear, turn against a society which — as they see it — patently has no interest in them.

2.2.2 *Social and life skills*

The simple division, however, of young people into the employed and unemployed fails to take into account that some young people will move from one category to the other haphazardly on the basis of whether, at any given time, they have a specific marketable asset or not. Thus, many of those consulted stressed the necessity of equipping these, and indeed all young people, to manage by themselves in these difficult circumstances. Dr. Morris Kaufmann of the Rubber and Plastics Processing Industry Training Board, for example, has been particularly influential in encouraging schools, colleges and other agencies to help equip the un- or under-qualified to cope, particularly though not exclusively, during a period of unemployment.

This very notion of 'coping' has drawn attention to what some regard as the new curricular area of 'social and life skills'. At the root of the discussions which are now taking place about the nature of this form of social education and the most appropriate methods of encouraging its acquisition, is the belief that most people lack the ability to stand back from the events they are participating in every day, to observe and analyse them. Geoffrey Melling, Director of the Further Education Curriculum Review and Development Unit, sees the basic elements of social education as "learning how to understand and anticipate how to act in social situations, and learning how to act oneself in an increasingly wide range of social contexts." The desirability of achieving this capacity for flexible response by young people faced with an uncertain and constantly changing future is obvious. Unfortunately agreement about its desirability is not matched by certainty about how to set about achieving it.

As was suggested in Chapter 1, young people struggling to achieve an independent adult status feel the need to experiment by trying out new types of social situations. What was being discussed by those of our informants concerned with developing 'social and life skills' approaches, is how young people can best be encouraged to widen their experiences constructively and to acquire the ability to learn from these experiences. This is, however, much more easily said than done and for many of our informants social and life skills were equated with much more tangible and straightforward tasks. The Distributive Industry Training Board, an organisation which has done much in developing fresh approaches to young people, argued, in a letter to the IBA's 16—19 Working Party in 1977, that there was a need for broadcast programmes

> "which would give information about where to go to find a job, whom to contact, how to write a letter of application, what to do before an interview, how to decide to take the job offered . . ."

Another ITB believed that programmes could usefully

> ". . . introduce the deductions from gross pay the employee experiences, such as income tax and national insurance and thus how social security benefits are funded . . ."

Mike Scally of the Counselling and Careers Development Unit at Leeds University felt that a 'personal survival and growth kit' was needed, related to decision making, crises coping, self-help, information finding and so on.

An important dimension of 'coping' or 'life skills' mentioned by young people was money management, especially the problems of learning to come to terms with the inelasticity of the weekly wage packet. One Leeds boy put it this way,

> "You don't realise how fast your money goes and where, and then you realise you are becoming in debt — the more money you earn, the more you are in debt somehow."

23

Money problems seemed particularly acute for boys in the 16–19 age group and were often linked to the wish to buy the most powerful motor bike possible!

2.2.3 *Basic education*

Social and life skills are clearly a key element in any basic education package. Other skills are also required. Indeed, there has been extensive discussion over the last two years about the ability of schools to produce young people equipped with such basic skills, particularly literacy and numeracy. The Prime Minister's Ruskin College speech in October 1976, the subsequent 'Great Debate' and the House of Commons Enquiry into *The Attainment of the School Leaver*, all have been expressions of this concern. The demands of an increasingly complex society put fresh pressures on the schools and by and large they are responding to these needs. Of course there is still room for improvement, if only arising from a better understanding of what is required. But it is being increasingly accepted that for a variety of reasons schools cannot be expected to equip everybody by the age of sixteen with all the basic skills for life. Thus, post-compulsory education, too, must look to the development of appropriate strategies of basic education. Adult, post-school, basic education has thus become for many people *the* new priority. Those who seek to dismiss it as yet another bandwagon might ponder a remark made by Professor H A Jones who, while commenting on the difficulty of giving a precise definition of 'adult basic education,' said it might best be described as "that bit of education without which there was no foundation to start building".

Significantly, the young people interviewed by IFF, whilst not expressing their basic education needs in the same ways as the adult professionals, nevertheless recognised that there were basic skills — literacy, numeracy, social and life skills were mentioned — which they needed to acquire even before they could obtain their first job. In particular they were concerned about how to cope with, and prepare for, interviews; television, they suggested, could help here. It was suggested also that television programmes could give advice on how to find out more about the firms one was applying to and what the real requirements of the jobs offered to young people actually were.

2.2.4 *Careers education*

Most young people, though, and most of the adults spoken to during the course of the Study, saw basic education provision principally in terms of the young person's ability to get a job. Indeed, although the process of selecting and obtaining a job is made infinitely easier by the acquisition of adequate levels of literacy, numeracy and social skills, the other essential element is an awareness by young people of the nature of working life itself, the range of jobs available and what each consists of. This basic 'careers education' was frequently mentioned as an area of need by many young people, particularly for those with minimal qualifications for whom a 'job' may well be a more realistic goal than a 'career'.

Almost everyone spoken to during the Study, and certainly young people and employers, felt that 'careers' provision is to say the least, patchy. There is a large gap between the reality and the ideal that is implicit in the definition given by the DES Survey 18 on *Careers Education*,

> "That element in the school programme more especially concerned with preparation for living and working in the adult world."

There is no doubt that in many cases 'careers' is still seen by the school to be a peripheral activity, and the staff involved given the minimum of time and resources to provide information and advice. The weaknesses in the existing pattern of provision have been well documented.[1]

Many of those in the Local Authority Careers Service also were aware that the shortage of staff and resources, coupled with the acute pressures created in many areas by the steep rise in youth unemployment, has meant that a less than satisfactory service is being provided to first time job-seekers. The effect of this pressure of work on an over-stretched service is compounded (in the view of many of our informants) by the Careers Service itself, which has not fully adjusted to the rapidly changing social and economic realities into which young people are being turned loose. This is a point made too by Ashton and Field and mentioned in the previous Chapter. It is only fair to add that

---

1 Those who would like more evidence might look at the House of Commons' Reports on *The Attainment of the School Leaver* (1977) and *People and Work* (1978)

many careers officers would reply that at a time when jobs are hard to get they are the easiest people to blame.

Nevertheless, many employers feel that young people leave school with little idea of the adult life that lies ahead of them or of the nature of the work they will be undertaking. It would be a mistake to assume that employers want the image of industry glamourized. Some do, but very far from all. They feel that careers films are not usually realistic. A Leeds employer said,

> "We were asked by the BBC if they could do a production of a careers film, and they spent one or two days filming the activities of a typical apprentice. It looked great — what . . . a terrific fulfilling job this was. It didn't show the poor little buggers clutching their heads and thinking, 'Ah — what's a quarter of a half?' And it didn't show the dirty side of the job."

The young people, too, claimed to want realism. They said they wanted to know what a job was really like — all the boring parts, the physical details of the job in terms of noise, whether you are standing up or sitting down, what breaks you get and when, what the hours were, what sort of people you would be working with, how closely supervised you would be and so on. One London girl describing why she liked the *London Weekend Show*, a local teenage current affairs/features programme produced by LWT, alleged that they would

> ". . . explain everything . . . if she was sitting there filing her nails they would show it, they don't hide anything; it's all out in the open even the boring bits like going to the toilet. They would probably say she'd just gone. They're like that . . ."

However, although young people and employers alike felt that the dirt, noise and monotony in any industrial job should not be hidden, neither should the compensations — aspects of factory life that were rarely communicated in careers pamphlets. A Swansea employer put it this way,

> "I mean one thing that industry has going for it which school hasn't very often is the camaraderie, I mean there is a hell of a good atmosphere in many of our sections. There is a hell of a family there — now that is the one big thing that industry has got going for it which doesn't really show up on any of the technical films which you see produced. There is so much humour on the shop floor."

26

Most adult groups, other than employees, were less sanguine — though they too called for greater realism. Generally it was felt that careers education had for too long been seen in terms of 'I want to be an X'. This was now changing from an emphasis on 'jobs' towards a wider appreciation of the problems of adult life. This trend looks towards a form of careers education that, Tony Watts, Director of the National Institute of Careers Education and Counselling (NICEC) has described as equipping

> "students with the skills, concepts and information they need in order to define who they are, who they want to be and assess how to relate to the total community."

Careers education in this sense is not just the concern of the school. Indeed, every year, some 9 million people change jobs. Consequently many of those consulted have argued that careers education and guidance should be a central plank in any process of continuing education. However, the following snippet of school-boy conversation, reported in *Lads, Lobes and Labour* by Paul Willis, hints at how difficult it might be in practice to reach the most disadvantaged young people — a group Willis describes as 'The Lads'.

> "Perc: I wonder why there's never kids like us in films to see what our attitude is to work.
> Fuzz: They're all Ear'oles
> Perc: All goody-goodies . . ."

2.2.5 *Alternatives to employment*

Many of those consulted during the Study argued that if, as they believe, unemployment is structural then it will be increasingly necessary for society to think about alternatives to employment. A paper prepared some time ago by Jim Radford of the Manchester Council for Voluntary and Social Service on *Inner Cities Unemployment*, points to difficulties in realising the opportunities.

> "Most of the information, advice and support that a group of unemployed people would need to start a small firm or co-operative venture is available now, but from many different sources, and the task of collecting and combining that information can be a lengthy and difficult one."

Co-operative ventures — even if modest — have been suggested by many individuals during the course of the Study, also the establishment of small businesses — window cleaning was the most often quoted example. The impression that we have been given, however, is that ideas for small business are difficult to put into practice. John Morrison, Principal Careers Officer for Fife, is very interested in the creation of small scale co-operative industrial ventures, but advised extreme caution to those who would imply that setting up a successful co-operative can be done easily and without outside help. Despite such difficulties there is clearly a need for alternatives to employment, paid and non-paid (many people mentioned community service) to be more fully explored.

2.2.6 *Community education*

The notion that the Government should support and develop various schemes which might conveniently be grouped under the umbrella heading of 'community education' was also mentioned. Other countries have considerable experience in this area, particularly those schemes in which young people are encouraged to develop their own projects. An example of this is seen in the Local Initiatives programme in Canada where the Government funded young artists, provided grants and advisory and training support for self enterprise, co-operatives, training workshops, and supported job creation projects based on community needs devised by young people themselves.

The community education element in the Youth Opportunities Programme now allows for the development of such possibilities here. The MSC has now made a decision to offer funding to various 'community agencies', principally for activities linked to their special programmes. The Scottish Community Education Centre, the Community Projects Foundation, the National Youth Bureau and the National Council for Social Service, for example, are all in receipt of, or will shortly receive, MSC funding for the development of various community projects such as training workshops, community service resources units and service schemes for youth workers. Such developments look promising for the future.

It is interesting to note, too, that various community initiatives in the UK — notably Northern Ireland — are already well established. In the case of Northern Ireland, some of these are supported by the Department of Manpower Services. Not only does there appear to be considerable grass roots activity in the development of, for example, work experience schemes, but also there are well established direct links between the Department of Manpower Services and community groups, for instance Community Service Volunteers in 'Young Help'. This leads one to wonder, in the light of the current developments and spirit of co-operation between the MSC and the community agencies noted above, what more adventurous community plans might be possible in the rest of the UK under the aegis of the MSC, given the goodwill of all parties.

2.2.7 *Political, social and economic understanding*

A feeling expressed by a large number of youth workers, teachers and others was that young people need more education in political matters. The Working Party of the Hansard Society's *Programme for Political Education* defined 'political literacy' as

> " ... the knowledge, skills and attitudes needed to make a man or woman informed about politics; able to participate in public life and groups of all kinds, both occupational and voluntary; and to recognise and tolerate diversities of political and social values ..."

and stated that

> ' ... a politically literate people should know what the main political disputes are about, how they are likely to affect them, how to relate to institutions, and they will have a predisposition to try to be politically effective while respecting the sincerity of others."

Many of those consulted during this Study thought that the need for political education was even more pressing than Hansard statements indicate. The National Front's policy of recruiting youngsters of fourteen into their youth wing was quoted more than once. Others, whilst not referring specifically to this development, drew our attention to what they saw as the growing political apathy in all sections of the community and what they feared to be the break-up of our democratic institutions. Hopefully, the DES circular 74/77 has paved the way towards a wider discussion of political matters, at least as far as educational institutions are concerned. It would, of course, be a mistake to think of political education solely in terms of the formal schools and colleges curriculum. The DES itself seems to recognise the need for political education outside the school curriculum, and has recently made a grant to the British Youth Council to encourage that organisation to act as a forum, and perhaps in the long term to set up youth councils in which young people might gain political experience.

Closely linked to the stated need for a greater political awareness on the part of young people and to the need for an understanding of the specific background to current economic and social situations in relation to unemployment, is the widely held belief that young people need to know much more about the nature and workings of industrial life. In their booklet *Understanding British Industry* the CBI says,

> "There remains a clear need for a more positive contribution through the normal processes of general education towards giving young people the opportunity to learn about the nature and functions of industry and of commerce, their social and economic contributions and the basic elements of business economics."

This need for 'understanding industrial society', as it is frequently described, seems broadly accepted in almost every quarter of industry and education. The TUC, for example, in their paper *16–18: The First Steps* looks to a development within schools of an education which prepares young people more generally for working life. The Schools Council is another body currently concerned with this need to develop an understanding of the industrial nature of our society in the minds of young people. The aim of the Schools Council Industry Project is

> ". . . to introduce into the education of young people, from the age of 13, an awareness and understanding of industry and its contribution to social, economic and cultural life."

It goes on to say that,

> "The accomplishment of this aim will depend upon the development of a sense of partnership, at both national and local levels, between participants from education and industry, so that both are better informed about each other's work and are fully involved in creating effective relationships."

It is interesting to note that the structure of the present project has been worked out in consultation with a planning group composed of representatives from the TUC, the CBI and education.

30

2.2.8 *Education for leisure*

The topic of leisure was mentioned by only a few of our informants. It may be that this was simply a reflection of our terms of reference which emphasised the transition from school to work rather than the broader general topic of transition from school to adult life. On the other hand, the relatively rare references to the importance of education for leisure may say something about the centrality of the work ethos in our society. It is perhaps significant that those of our informants who did mention the great importance of leisure and the active preparation for it, did so very strongly and always in the context of the urgent need to recognise that today's young people will grow older in a world in which paid work, where it exists, will take up fewer and fewer hours in each week. Significantly, comments about the need for more active leisure provision came particularly from those geographical areas where unemployment has been a problem for generations: in Northern Ireland, for example. The future they claimed requires, as never before, that young people become as self-reliant as possible in making the most satisfying and fulfilling use of their leisure time.

In Northern Ireland, schemes to help the young unemployed frequently feature the development of self-reliance in leisure. In other parts of the UK too, the importance of such preparation was also stressed. Some argued that the effect of mass entertainment media has been to limit most people's capacity for active participation in leisure pursuits and, conversely, to increase the extent of passive or spectator involvement. Compared with previous generations, some argued, young people generally have less idea of how to cope with time if thrown on their own resources. This may or may not be true with regard to past generations, but future generations will certainly be required to occupy themselves for longer periods of time than has been the case in the past.

2.2.9 *Relationships*

Of other areas of need highlighted during the course of the Study, frequent reference was made to changing and developing sexual relationships. The young people interviewed by IFF mentioned, in particular, the effects of their changing relationships with their parents during the period of transition. The parents were seen as finding it difficult to accept their children's newly ac-

31

quired role as adult wage-earner or, just as importantly, to accept the problems they had in finding jobs. For their part, the young people found it difficult to communicate their feelings or explain the situation they found themselves in. This is an area in which girls appear to have greater problems than boys.

2.2.10 *YOP and UVP*

Over and above the specific subject areas (of which basic education, including numeracy, literacy and social and life skills, together with careers education and the problems of unemployment were most frequently mentioned,) explicit and frequent reference was made to the opportunities afforded for innovative curriculum development in many of the above areas within the context of the MSC's Youth Opportunities Programme and the development of the joint DES/MSC Unified Vocational Peparation scheme. Indeed, although UVP schemes were frequently criticised, they served to emphasise what many of our consultants saw as a key factor, namely, that the extent of youth unemployment should not blind us to the fact that many young people who are in employment have little or no access to further education and training, and that their needs will in most instances be identical to those of their unemployed companions.

2.3 Special categories of need

Two other categories were singled out by numbers of our informants as requiring particular attention in an assessment of needs. One group comprises recent or first generation immigrants to this country. The other group is the female half of the population.

2.3.1 Immigrants in any society are always at the greatest disadvantage. They are less likely to have an understanding of how the society operates, how to communicate appropriately and often in an unfamiliar tongue, how to conform to accepted norms of behaviour. Added to which, in times of economic recession when 'last-in, first-out' operates, they are likely to be first to suffer the hardship of unemployment. Add to this, in the case of those whose family origin is the Caribbean or the Indian sub-Continent, the existence of overt racial prejudice in the selection of employees — the claims of this group to be treated as a 'special case' appeared to many of our informants to be overwhelming. But perhaps the chief reason and cause for particular concern is the plight of those of Caribbean origin living in decayed inner city areas. The absence of jobs and social and cultural amenities and the presence of racial prejudice have resulted, in the view of our informants from the West Indian community, in a very marked degree of alienation among young blacks from sources of official 'white' help. Provision for young blacks is only likely to be effective, therefore, if provided within an 'all-black' context. If this is so, it has profound implications for the role of broadcasting.

2.3.2 Girls are hardly a minority group. Yet many people certainly saw them as being seriously disadvantaged. In comparison with boys there were many more restricting preconceptions about the sorts of opportunities in education and employment which were appropriate to girls. These preconceptions affected the attitudes of parents, teachers, employers and careers staff, and not surprisingly, the girls themselves. As a result, at a time when much stress was being placed on the need to obtain skills and qualifications, girls were still nowhere near as much in evidence on courses in colleges or on vocational training schemes. In a time of rapid social and economic change generally, there is less and less room for traditional views about women's roles. In addition to all the other needs listed above, girls need to be helped to overcome these traditional restrictions. Marriage must no longer be thought of as a terminal occupation.

2.4 Not everyone who reads this Report will agree with all the expressions of need outlined so far in this Chapter. Some people in the education, careers and youth services may even be irritated on the grounds that they are already well aware of the needs and are responding as fully as they can, given frequently limited resources. But the points noted do represent the major concerns of the majority of our informants.

2.5 The needs of adult groups

2.5.1 The adults, the professionals, who formed the main group of those consulted during the Study, were, of course, by comparison with almost all the young people interviewed, distinctly advantaged, articulate and well-educated. However, they too felt that they needed support and help which might be offered by the media in general, and broadcasting in particular.

33

2.5.2 Various people expressed the need for a new range of in-service training opportunities for teachers and lecturers both in schools and in colleges; amongst them was George Tolley, Chairman of the Further Education Curriculum Review and Development Unit. The training would, of course, be related to new trends in the curriculum and, for example, might involve careers education and appreciation of industry and commerce for those in schools, while those in further education might require help in coping with the demands of MSC-inspired initiatives.

2.5.3 Indeed, some further education lecturers and others concerned with the development of the YOP chose to stress that, from September 1978, large numbers of staff would be faced with the need to provide an 'opportunity' for young people. It was felt that many lecturers/tutors would be faced, perhaps for the first time (despite ATTI and NATFHE statements which have argued that technical colleges have always dealt with the full ability range of young people,) with a type of unmotivated youngster who, whilst instantly recognisable to any inner-city school teacher, has not in the past found his or her way into further education. There is serious concern that any attempt to use the traditional college teaching methods with this essentially new clientele will have disastrous consequences. A recent survey of provision for the young unemployed carried out by the FECRDU comments that few colleges referred to in-service training — despite the obvious need for it.

> "The staff of many of these courses had to comprehend the roles of manager (developing the programme, maintaining contact with sponsoring agencies and local firms, recruiting young people and helping with job placements), counsellor (advising applicants to the course, boosting their confidence, assessing their strengths and weaknesses in relation to skill acquisition and employment, and helping to resolve problems of a personal nature), and teacher (not only of straight subject content but often through the medium of 'experimental' learning in which in-course objectives were included in projects, simulations, work observations and work experience)."

2.5.4 There are, of course, some interesting examples of non-traditional work going on with young disadvantaged people within the colleges of further education at the moment. These include Tottenham Technical College, the South Thames College and City and East London. Tottenham, for example, has developed its own unit for disadvantaged young people. This unit has its own learning styles with an emphasis on self-pacing and on strong personal links between staff and students. A similar approach is being carried out in Coventry where the LEA's pioneering use of the Old Fire Station has attracted considerable attention.

2.5.5 The only reservation that some people expressed about in-service provision for further education lecturers in relation to their new YOP responsibilities, was that such specialist provision might not necessarily be used by those who were in most need of it. Such people argued that what was needed was not in-service education but more resource material – an argument which could well be applied to in-service work with schools groups too – so that the tutors, teachers and lecturers would be introduced to good quality material and would thus indirectly participate in some sort of in-service training.

2.5.6 Many people, too, referred to the role that adults generally could play in relation to meeting the needs of young people. Some people specifically mentioned the notion, originally developed by John Bazalgette of the Grubb Institute, of a 'working coach'. A related, though different, theme is taken up by Morris Kaufmann of the Rubber and Plastics Processing Industry Training Board, who has written on various occasions about the informal role of adults in industry as, in his terminology, 'industrial tutors'. The common fact behind these ideas is that most young people (especially girls) entering industry or commerce not only have few or no opportunities for further education or training, but also are rarely inducted into general aspects of industrial life: clocking on and off, trade union activities and so on. The coach or tutor idea recognises the important role which adults can play in helping young people to understand their place of work. In essence it is about 'sitting with Nellie', though not in any narrow sense of learning one specific process, but rather in the broader sense of being inducted into the adult working world generally. The hope is that the young person next to Nellie, as it were, will thus be better able with her guidance to make the transition from the dependence of school to the independence of the workplace. We know there are large number of adults who, doubtless unconsciously, are already filling the coach/tutor role with greater or lesser success. It may be that such a role best operates on an informal, unconscious level and that any attempt to formalise it

35

would be counter-productive. We can only comment that a substantial number of people thought otherwise and considered that
help and training would be needed by those designated, however
informally, as coaches and tutors, if they were to be able to help
young people to the best of their capabilities.

2.5.7 Many of these workers who informally induct young people
into adult working life are, of course, parents. It was suggested
that helping parents to help young people should be a priority
both with regard to information about education and training
opportunities and about broader social, political and economic
changes which were setting a life context for their children vastly
different from the era in which they grew up and started work.
In particular, it was felt that parents frequently had little idea
of the aims and objectives of the school curriculum, or of the significance of subject choices for fourth-formers from the point
of view of career decisions, and so on. Similarly, it was claimed
that parents were unaware of the possible opportunities for their
children in further education or training, or, if unemployed, what
opportunities were offered in the Government 'special programmes', YOP and STEP. This lack of appreciation is, of course, particularly acute in the case of those parents who also happen to be
employers and who might be willing to offer young people YOP
places if they knew more about the special programmes, for
example.

2.5.8 In addition to these comments about parental lack of information in relation to matters concerning education and employment, many also felt that parents were very often ill-equipped
to handle other aspects of the young person's transition from
school to adulthood. John Bazalgette quoted research that shows
that whereas the so-called 'common sense' notion is that young
people do not value their parents' opinions highly, in fact the
reverse is true. He argues that not only are young people concerned about their parents' perception of them in all aspects of
their life, but also that the parents themselves are greatly concerned about their 'transitional' youngsters but don't know how
to help in a way that is acceptable. Something which helps explore
these issues and relationships would do much to help parents and
young people.

2.5.9 It is interesting to consider how broadcast provision to meet these needs might also provide the common ground between 'helpers' and 'helped', between young people and adult groups. Many of those spoken to during the course of the Study identified certain key areas of needs, and in almost all cases they felt that broadcasting on its own or, as will be explored in the next Chapter, in co-operation with other agencies, has a major role to play in helping young adults and professional groups alike.

3   Young adults and the media

3.0 So far in this part of the Report we have looked at the young people themselves and their needs as they make the transition from school to work. This Chapter looks at what is known about the mass media, particularly broadcasting, specifically in relation to young people aged 14–21, and points up a lack of adequate research in this area. The information we have been able to gather about the use made of television and radio set out in this Chapter is also referred to in other sections of the Report and helped to inform and support our conclusions and recommendations. However, it is detailed at some length here because of its intrinsic interest and also because it might form the basis of a subsequent enquiry.

3.1 We realise that the information presented in this Chapter is less than perfect, and even where it exists (for print, television or radio) the bases differ wildly and the data itself is often superficial. For example, details of readership fail to reveal differences between those in their early teens and those in their early twenties and exclude those members of the public who are in socio-economic group E.* Moreover, the surveys quoted are hardly comparable since they are based on different samples and were conducted at different times. Additionally, how does one compare, say, average exposure (in hours per week) to television with a figure for the percentage of young adults who have looked at a specified newspaper during the seven days prior to interview? Over and above all these problems, 'young adults' may mean 15–19 years in one survey and 15–24 in another.

3.2 In short, an informed statement about the media use of those

---

* See Glossary

aged between 14 and 21 years could only be based upon an empirical study which has yet to be conducted. Needless to say, we know less about 'disadvantaged' young adults than about young adults in general. Similarly, many academic studies have excluded girls, and commercial investigations financed by advertisers and manufacturers are unlikely to pay much attention to those with the least economic weight. Predictions of the media behaviour of specified groups of young people, say, 14–17 years old, female and city dwellers, may almost as well be based on intuition as on existing data.

3.3 A recently published survey of the expenditure patterns, life styles and attitudes of young adults has the apt title, *You Don't Know Me*.[1] With only a few exceptions, studies of how, why and when people use mass media have ignored those in the age range 14 to 21 years, yet these are important years during which new patterns of media-use are forming. After a childhood in which television is the most dominant, in some cases the only mass medium, young adults reduce the amount of time spent viewing, and print, records, radio and cinema become increasingly attractive as the child approaches adulthood.

3.4 To understand, even in part, the role of media in young adults' lives, we need to create a comprehensive picture of media-use patterns and of assumptions about media, although even this is not enough. To study media in isolation is to risk gaining misleading impressions unless it is set in its social context.

3.5 Therefore, to explore the media we must also explore the day-to-day lives of those who use them. Academics and the media themselves have shown considerable interest in minority youth groups — skinheads, bootboys, bikeboys, mods, rockers, juvenile prostitutes, junkies, delinquents and football hooligans (and all should be in quotation marks) — but the ordinary sixteen or seventeen year old gains scant attention, which reflects a general attitude to the population at large. Thus, not only do we know little about young adults, but also the images we present to young adults *of themselves* are often anti-social rigid stereotypes.

---

1 *You Don't Know Me* – A Survey of Youth in Britain – McCann Erickson Ltd – 1977

3.6 The scope of this Study does not allow discussion of the parts played by adult anxiety and disenchantment or the role of 'newsworthiness' in the generation and acceptance of unfortunate images of youth, but it would be foolish to ignore the fact that young adults are searching for new, non-childlike identities and that the contribution of certain media on certain occasions to this quest is the distribution of unrealistic images.

3.7 Following these generalisations, the remainder of this Chapter details information generated by relatively sound research which is relevant to young adults and media. We end with a brief note on theoretical issues and a strong recommendation that an empirical study on this area be mounted as soon as possible.

3.8 Television

3.8.1 A study conducted in the early sixties found that when a family bought their first television set the total amount of time the family spent together was unchanged.[1] There was one exception to this general finding: bringing television into the home seemed to push the teenagers out. Perhaps it is significant that the term 'teenagers' appears to have originated in the fifties when television began its attack on the time between working and sleeping.

3.8.2 Teenagers, or young adults, devote roughly 9% of their week to watching television. Although this is a substantial period of viewing, it is less than for any other age group. In contrast, at 12–14 years viewing is peaking for working class boys at an average of 24 hours per week.[2] The exact nature of the dip, even the location of the age at which viewing is at a minimum, has never been recorded.

3.8.3 On a general basis we can conclude that viewing is a seasonal activity influenced by demographic factors such as age, sex and social class. Similarly, boys spend more time with television than do girls, but women are heavier viewers than men. Table 1 shows

1 Belson, W A – *The Impact of Television* – Crosby, Lockwood – 1967

2 Greenberg, B S – Viewing and Listening: Parameters among British Youngsters – in R Brown (Ed.) – *Children and Television* – Collier Macmillan: Sage – 1976

the effect of sex and social class on viewing for 12—19 year olds, and the dramatic dip in viewing is noticeable.

Table 1: Average daily exposure to television (hours and minutes): sex within class within age (1971)[1]

	12 — 14 years		15 — 19 years	
	Middle Class	Working Class	Middle Class	Working Class
Male	3:01	3:22	2:01	2:06
Female	2:48	2:48	1:56	2:13

The table shows a fall in viewing with age and an interaction between sex and class can be noted; at 12—14 years working class girls were still viewing less than working class boys but by 15—19 years this has been reversed. The changeover for members of the middle class occurs later.

3.8.4 Of course, the majority of young adults live with their parents and thus many have restrictions imposed on their viewing. In fact slightly under half of 15—17 year olds have viewing deadlines which come from parents rather than their own inclinations.[2]

3.8.5 In addition, it should not be forgotten that many young people have access to television programmes in their schools and 'schools television' is used in more than one third of UK secondary schools. But it must be emphasised that to know the number of schools, or classes, that 'take' a schools broadcast tells us nothing about how the broadcast is used by the school, by the teacher, by the class or by the individual pupil — it is a quantitative rather than a qualitative analysis.

3.8.6 After all that — *what does the young adult watch on television?* A first split is in terms of the three available channels. Here the complexity increases. At 10—14 years both boys and girls are slightly more likely to be watching BBC 1 than ITV, by 20—25 years the majority of women are viewing ITV and some

---

1 Greenberg, B S op cit

2 Carrick James Market Research — *A National Survey of 7—17 year olds —* Jan/Feb 1978

12% of men claim to be watching BBC 2 most often. The figures are detailed in Table 2. They arise from the *claimed* behaviour of young people in answer to the question, "which channel do you watch most often?" Other ways of collecting these data might produce different patterns. (And, like all survey questions, this one is open to interpretation: Is the channel you view 'most often' the one that you spend the greatest amount of time watching? Does, for example, 'view' mean watch attentively or occasionally glance at a programme that someone else wishes to see?)

Table 2: Television channel preferences by age and sex (1978)[1]

		10—14 yrs	15—19 yrs	20—25 yrs
BBC 1	Male	66%	51%	43%
	Female	54%	43%	45%
BBC 2	Male	2%	2%	12%
	Female	—	1%	1%
ITV	Male	30%	41%	41%
	Female	43%	52%	50%
Equal	Male	2%	5%	5%
	Female	2%	6%	3%

Another way of considering channel preference is to consider the number of programmes issuing from each channel which achieve high penetration of the age group. In an average winter week during 1976 some 43 programmes were seen by over 20% of those over 15 years. Only 34 programmes had 20% or more penetration of the young adult group (in this case defined as 15—19 year olds). Of the 34 high penetration programmes 18 were screened by ITV, 14 by BBC 1 and 2 by BBC 2.[2]

3.8.7 Turning to the types of programmes most regularly watched by young adults (and here the definition becomes 15—17 years), sex differences emerge. Tables 3 and 4 show the types of programme most regularly viewed and the types of programme most frequently nominated as favourites by 15—17 year olds. The tables

---

1 Unpublished data from *You Don't Know Me* survey — McCann Erickson
2 BBC Audience Research Department — *Viewing by Age, Sex and Class* — 1978

are taken from a 1978 survey and based upon self-reports by young people.

Table 3: Types of television programmes watched regularly by the majority of young adults[1]

	Male	Female
Pop music programmes	59%	75%
News broadcasts	52%	35%
Action thrillers	77%	81%
Cartoons	58%	52%
Sport	72%	28%

Table 4: Types of television programmes most frequently nominated as favourites[1]

	Male	Female
Pop music	51%	61%
Action thrillers	68%	69%
Sports programmes	62%	10%
Westerns	25%	11%
Hollywood musicals	2%	30%
Romantic drama	2%	23%
Documentaries	24%	17%
Cartoons	25%	21%

3.8.8 Here is the first hint that the programmes most frequently viewed are not necessarily the programmes that are most appreciated. There is greater difference between the sexes in Table 4, but sex differences are also apparent in Table 3. Sport is an obvious area. Since much sports coverage occurs at well defined, regular times it can be sought out by interested viewers (male — 72%) and avoided by others (female — 28%). But why should young women view news broadcasts less regularly than do young men (52% — 35%)? Do they switch off (mentally) when the news comes on? Are they sent to make reviving drinks whilst serious minded males keep up with world affairs?

3.8.9 In the same survey respondents were asked to nominate their three favourite television programmes. Table 5 shows all programmes that were listed first, second or third by 10% or

1 Carrick James op. cit

43

more of respondents aged between 15 and 17 years.

Table 5: Programmes nominated 1st, 2nd or 3rd favourites by 10% or more
(January 1978)[1]

	Male	Female
Match of the Day	19%	1%
World of Sport/Sports	19%	2%
Starsky and Hutch	15%	32%
Happy Days	10%	15%
The Sweeney	13%	7%
Top of the Pops	12%	30%
Crossroads	6%	31%
Charlie's Angels	3%	10%
Coronation Street	2%	13%

Starsky and Hutch, Top of the Pops and *Crossroads* were most
frequently nominated by girls while boys preferred *World of
Sport* and *Match of the Day*. There is more uniformity of preference amongst girls than boys. No programme was nominated
by more than 19% of boys whilst three programmes gained
nominations by 30% or more girls. It is at least possible that
this uniformity of preference is a consequence of a relative dearth
of television characters and situations with which girls can identify.

3.8.10 Respondents were also asked to nominate their three favourite television personalities. Table 6 lists all personalities nominated
by 10% boys or girls.

Table 6: Television personalities nominated 'favourite' by 10% of young
adults (January 1978)[1]

	Male	Female
Starsky	4	25
Hutch	5	19
Starsky and Hutch	11	16
Noel Edmunds	5	18
Henry Winkler	10	10
Morecambe and Wise	18	7
The Two Ronnies	10	5
Ronnie Barker	10	3

1 Carrick James, op. cit.

Table 6 Cont.

The Sweeney	10	12
Charlie's Angels	23	19
Jill Monroe	13	5
Bionic Woman	17	15
Angela Rippon	11	3
Penelope Keith	4	15

Although there are some cross-overs from Table 5 which lists favourite programmes, it is noticeable that favourite programmes do not of necessity feature favourite characters. *Crossroads* for instance was nominated favourite by 30% of girls, but no characters from *Crossroads* appear in Table 6. Instead the list seems to consist of personalities most of whom might be characterised as young middle-aged, laid-back/cool and/or humorous. But such imposed assumptions are at best arrogant – in order to understand the appeal of 'favourites' it would be necessary to hear young people discuss them further.

3.9 Radio

3.9.1 Like television viewing, radio listening is a seasonal activity. And like viewing, listening can to some small extent be predicted on the basis of demographic characteristics: age, sex and social grade.

3.9.2 The interaction of demographic factors and season, however, is rather more complex for radio than television. Indeed radio itself is a more diverse medium than television, offering greater choice of station for longer periods of the day. Most radio listeners can – though few do – receive Radio 1, Radio 2, Radio 3, Radio 4, one or more BBC Local Radio stations, one or more Independent Local Radio Stations, plus a profusion of foreign stations. And, to add a little more complexity, many listeners (almost a half of all male young adults), own cassette or tape recorders and are able to record off-air and replay radio broadcasts whenever they choose. (Just short of 2½ million blank tapes and cassettes per year are sold to girls aged 12 – 18 years, the figure for young men is not available.)[1]

---

1 International Publishing Corporation *Teenage Girls A Market Expenditure Study* – 1977

3.9.3 However, whilst young adults are less likely to watch television than any other age group, they are amongst the most heavily exposed to radio. (20—29 year olds are the heaviest listeners, young adults up to 20 form the second most heavily exposed group.) And whilst children are the most heavily exposed to television, they are the least heavily exposed to radio. On television 5—14 year olds listen for approximately 2—4 hours per week, 15—19 year olds roughly 9—11 hours.

3.9.4 Predictably, young people are more likely than any other group to tune into 'music' stations. A recent survey showed that average listening to non 'pop' music stations (Radio 3, Radio 4, BBC Local Radio) amongst young adults totals 23 minutes per week out of an average weekly exposure of 10 hours 54 minutes. In other words roughly 10½ hours per week was spent listening to ILR, Radio 1 and Radio 2 (and only 53 minutes of this went to Radio 2).[1]

3.9.5 Comparing the audiences for local radio with those for national radio is difficult. An average national audience for local radio, whilst not meaningless, bears little resemblance to the reality of local radio listening. And even generalisations from local station to local station have very limited validity. But it is clear that a young adult who lives in an area which is served by BBC Local Radio and ILR is more likely to prefer the latter.[2] With the future spread of local radio this means that for most young adults the choice will be between ILR and BBC Radio 1 and any attempt to reach young people through radio is likely to have the greatest direct impact by exploiting these two broadcasting channels. Further impact could also be gained by an indirect approach, for example, mothers of young adults could be reached via Radio 2 and BBC Local Radio. Indirect impact or the 'two-step' communications effect is discussed later in this Chapter.

3.9.6 Local radio deserves some special attention in the context of this Young Adult Study. Reference is made in the Study's terms of reference to the unemployed or disadvantaged young adult, and

1 BBC Audience Research Department — *Annual Review of BBC Research Findings* — 1977
2 ARD and JICRAR data

the majority of young people who fall into these categories (and the more tightly 'disadvantaged' is defined, the more valid is this statement) are city dwellers. Conditions vary from city to city. Local radio and other local media allow a flexible reaction to varying conditions, but this is not to say that national stations, Radio 1 in particular, can play no adequate part in broadcasting's service to young adults. Yet to exploit radio fully, national and local channels of communication should be used in quite different ways. Apart from local radio's greater flexibility of response and its ability to serve closely defined geographical areas, local radio also allows greater and more meaningful access to its listeners. A Radio 1 programme made 'by and for' young adults – admittedly not likely – would be a quite different creature to programmes *made to the same brief* by young adults using local radio facilities.

3.10 Cinema

3.10.1 According to *Social Trends* (No. 8, 1977), average weekly cinema attendance has dropped from 25 million in 1953 to approximately 2 million in 1976, but the decrease in attendance is *least marked* amongst 15–24 year olds. It seems to be beyond dispute that young adults are more likely to attend the cinema than any other age group. Table 7 is based on a survey conducted in 1975 and shows that whilst 9% of those interviewed were aged 15–19 years they formed 16% of those who occasionally attended the cinema and 28% of frequent cinema goers.

Table 7: Cinema attendance by age (1975)[1]

Age	Never	Rarely	Occasionally	Frequently	All
15–19	3	6	16	28	9
20–29	8	16	25	33	16
30–49	31	44	42	30	34
50+	58	34	17	9	41
	100%	100%	100%	100%	100%

Those in their twenties are also over-represented in the audience for cinema films (although to a lesser extent than young adults).

---

1 BBC Audience Research Department: *Summary of Recent Research into Cinema Going and Television Viewing* – 1975

It is likely that, once past adolescence, chronological age is replaced by domestic age (marital and parental status) as the best predictor of cinema going.

3.10.2 Little else of relevance is known about cinema attendance and the sex and class structure of a typical cinema audience varies according to different data sources. Although some analytical studies have explored the psychological appeal of, say, Westerns, no study has been located that details the content preferences of young adults.

3.11 Newspapers

3.11.1 During January and December 1977, some 37,000 adults were questioned about their newspaper and magazine reading habits in an annual study known as the *National Readership Survey*. The information in the following sections is taken from a further analysis of these data which gives detailed breakdowns of readership in terms of age, social grade and sex (*The Sunday Times Supplement to the National Readership Survey*, January – December 1977).

3.11.2 The survey revealed that 73% of the adult (15 years+) population of the UK read (during the 7 days prior to interview) one or more national daily newspapers; 42% read an evening paper; 83% a national Sunday paper. For young adults (15–24 years) the percentages are 76, 44 and 83 respectively. In other words, taken as a whole young adults are as likely to read newspapers as the average British adult.

3.11.3 The survey also reveals that national dailies reach 75% of young adult middle class (ABC1) males and 70% of young adult middle class females. Amongst the findings the survey reveals that young adults show average to above average readership of national, Sunday and regional newspapers. Young adult men are more likely to be readers than women, and members of the working classes are more likely to read a newspaper than are members of the middle classes.

3.11.4 The general trend for young adults to show average to above average readership of the national daily and weekly papers has six exceptions; the *Daily* and *Sunday Express*, the *Daily* and *Sunday Telegraph*, the *Daily Mail* and the *Financial Times*. Table 8 shows the readership of all national newspapers for young adults and all adults (including the 15−24 year old adults, therefore differences between 'young adults' and 'all adults' are smaller than if 'young adults' were compared with those of 25 years or older). In the context of disadvantaged young adults it should be noted that the working class percentages exclude socio-economic grade E which is defined as those on the lowest levels of subsistence.

Table 8: Readership of national newspapers: young adults (15−24 years) and all adults (15+) sex within social grade (1977)

	ABC 1				C2D			
	Male		Female		Male		Female	
	YA	All	YA	All	YA	All	YA	All
	%	%	%	%	%	%	%	%
The Sun	30	21	23	14	55	44	42	33
Daily Mirror	29	21	24	16	48	42	33	31
Daily Express	21	22	17	17	15	17	9	12
Daily Mail	19	19	17	16	10	12	8	9
Daily Telegraph	14	17	11	15	3	3	2	2
Daily Record	4	3	4	2	8	7	7	5
The Times	8	6	6	4	1	1	1	1
The Guardian	7	6	5	4	1	1	1	1
Financial Times	5	6	3	2	1	−	1	−
News of the World	20	20	24	16	46	45	42	39
Sunday People	24	20	21	17	41	36	33	33
Sunday Express	29	33	27	31	12	15	11	14
Sunday Post	9	8	9	8	14	13	13	13
Sunday Times	22	19	21	17	6	4	3	3
Sunday Telegraph	13	13	10	11	3	3	2	2
Sunday Mail	7	5	6	4	10	8	9	7
The Observer	14	11	12	10	3	3	2	2
Sunday Mirror	30	23	31	21	47	40	42	35

At least on the surface this evidence is quite unequivocal. Relative to the adult population as a whole young adults are more likely to see a newspaper than their elders. But it should be noted that 'readership' tells us nothing of how much time is spent in reading in any particular week.

3.12 Magazines

3.12.1 Information about the readership for magazines is taken from the same source as newspaper readership. Four major groupings of magazines are covered: General Weeklies, Women's Weeklies, General Monthlies and Women's Monthlies and inspection of Table 9 shows that as with newspapers, 15—24 year olds see more magazines than adults as a whole.

Table 9: Group readership for magazines, young adults compared with adult population as a whole (1977)

	Any General Weekly	Any Women's Weekly	Any General Monthly	Any Women's Monthly
Young adults (15—24)	65%	42%	48%	49%
Adult population (15+)	55%	37%	41%	42%

Needless to say considerable variation in readership of magazines is found when these figures are broken down by sex and class.

3.12.2 Whilst newspapers as a whole gain higher penetration of the C2D socio-economic groups, magazines gain higher penetration of the ABC1 socio-economic groups. Table 10 documents the readership of named magazines by young adults.

Table 10: Magazines most likely to be read by young adults (15—24 years) (1977)

	ABC1 Male	C2D Male	ABC1 Female	C2D Female
General Weeklies				
TV Times	32%	29%	35%	28%
Radio Times	34%	25%	37%	22%
Exchange and Mart	14%	14%	–	–
New Musical Express	22%	18%	10%	–
Melody Maker	20%	15%	–	–
The Weekly News	–	11%	–	14%
Weekend	–	12%	11%	11%
Women's Weeklies				
Woman's Own	–	–	42%	33%
Woman	–	–	42%	33%
Woman's Weekly	–	–	17%	16%
Woman's Realm	–	–	16%	14%
My Weekly	–	–	–	11%
Jackie	–	–	16%	22%
Loving	–	–	–	12%
Love Affair	–	–	–	10%

Table 10 Cont'd

General Monthlies				
Readers' Digest	26%	20%	28%	17%
Mayfair	14%	15%	–	–
Practical Motorist	–	13%	–	–
Men Only	10%	12%	–	–
Penthouse	–	12%	–	–
Car Mechanics	12%	15%	–	–
Motor Sport	14%	11%	–	–
Hot Car	17%	17%	–	–
Brides & Setting Home	–	–	10%	–
Woman & Home	–	–	14%	10%
Family Circle	–	–	17%	14%
Good Housekeeping	–	–	16%	–
Ideal Home	–	–	10%	–
Vogue	–	–	23%	12%
She	–	–	20%	10%
Living	–	–	14%	12%
Cosmopolitan	10%	–	29%	15%
True Romances	–	–	11%	19%
True Story	–	–	10%	17%
Woman's World	–	–	11%	–
Honey	–	–	18%	10%
'19'	–	–	22%	12%
Romance	–	–	–	13%
Over 21	–	–	17%	10%
Look Now	–	–	15%	10%
Argis:3*	–	–	16%	26%

(*True Romances, True Story, Women's Story : combined readership)

Significantly for the purposes of this Study, the two magazines most likely to be read by the greatest number of young adults are *Radio Times* and *TV Times*. (Of course other publications may be read more attentively or more exhaustively, as reading in this context may mean merely 'look at'.) It is also worth noting that the monthly *Reader's Digest* gains a readership of between 17 and 26% across *all* young adults interviewed. But a message directed towards women would have more chance of being received if placed in, for example, *Woman's Own* or *Woman*.

3.12.3 Readership details of the sort outlined above, however, fail to indicate the meanings that young adults, either as a whole or as defined sub-groups, attach to magazines. For example, we do not know which magazine specified groups of young people turn to for advice, images of appropriate dress, behaviour and identity.

3.12.4 It would be useful to know how such specified sub-groups of young people differ in their readership patterns and which parts of magazines are read with greatest attention, and by whom. Specialist magazines can reach minority groups, but because of low readership levels little is known about their readers. One small scale study, admittedly of limited methodological sophistication, analysed the readership of *Kung Fu Monthly*.[1] The estimated total readership of this magazine was 285,000, 69% of the readers were aged 15–21 years, 62% were male, 61% came from unskilled manual home backgrounds. But the most startling findings were concerned with the ethnic origins of readers. Only 27% of readers had parents born in the UK; 31% were of West Indian origin; 28% Asian and the remainder were mainly of Greek origin. Studies of this kind highlight the importance of a further research initiative in this area of young adults and the media.

3.13 Comics

3.13.1 Approximately sixty publications per week are directed at children and some of these are read by young adults. A major survey of the children's market conducted in 1970 revealed that 68% of 13–15 year olds were exposed to one or more of 28 advertisements carrying juvenile publications in an average week.[2] In a survey conducted for the IBA (1972) some 24% of 13–15 year olds claimed to have spent time reading a comic on the day before interview.[3] And a study conducted in Scottish schools for the National Foundation for Educational Research revealed that 13,842 thirteen year olds claimed to have read 11,483 comics, newspapers or magazines during the week prior to interview.[4]

It seems likely then that comics and juvenile magazines reach at least 50% of young adults in an average week.

---

1 Quoted in: Robins, D and Cohen, P – *Knuckle Sandwich* – Penguin Books – 1978

2 IPC – *The Children's Market* – 1970

3 IBA – *A Survey on the Relationship between Children and Television Phase I* – 1972

4 Maxwell, J – *Reading Progress from 8 to 15* – NFER Publishing Company – 1977

3.14 **Alternative press, freesheets, leaflets and posters**

These media are placed together because no firm information concerning exposure or readership has been located.

3.14.1 The majority of British cities now have their own alternative or community newspapers and it seems likely that young adults form a considerable proportion of their readership. The *Leeds Other Paper*, for example, reports a drop in circulation of almost 1,000 issues (approximately 50%) during college and university vacations. *LOP* is published fortnightly, but the majority of alternative papers are more spasmodic in their appearance on the streets. Several papers published by and for black minority groups are being organised under the umbrella of *Race Today*. The total readership of alternative publications is doubtless extremely small in comparison with national and regional newspapers. But the alternative press does offer a channel of communication with readers who are likely to be highly defined in terms of age, social class and geographical location – characteristics which are also salient in the definition of the young unemployed and disadvantaged.

3.14.2 Alternative newspapers are often produced by young 'journalists' with little or no background in the industry but with considerable drive and commitment. The need to feel close to those who produce (in a general sense) public communications is common enough, and many of those who run alternative papers, which sometimes have editorial areas of a few square miles, are also involved in community action, street politics and assorted community self-help and care projects. Although few alternative/community papers exemplify 'like communicating with like', they come closer to this particular ideal than any other medium. The extent of the authority and trustworthiness of these publications in the view of highly defined groups of young people has yet to be explored.

3.14.3 Evidence suggests that young adults form a disproportionately large section of the readership of national newspapers. It would seem likely, all other things being equal (which relatively they rarely are), that a fair sized proportion of young adults will read advertising freesheets when they are available, and it follows that their mobile life-style would expose them to posters and free leaflets.

3.15 A general note on communication and effects

3.15.1 How well a medium communicates a particular message depends upon characteristics of the message, the medium and the target audience. It is important to know what the purpose of the message is. Is it to change attitudes or behaviour? Is it to generate a specified emotion or to lodge certain information in the recipient's memory? What sensory modalities does the medium stimulate? Vision or hearing? Is the medium easily controlled (print) by its user? Or do a small number of people dictate how and when it can be used (television and radio)? How much does it cost to use the medium? And how does the user pay (television v cinema or books)? Is the medium on tap or must the potential user make special arrangements? And so on.

3.15.2 Similarly, what assumption does the potential recipient of the message bring to the medium? Do young people think of television mainly as a source of entertainment, films as providing an opportunity to gain bodily contact with the opposite (or same) sex and print as an arid educational medium?

3.15.3 In order to communicate a message to some particular section of the public, it is clearly desirable to use several media, breaking the message into component parts and carefully selecting an appropriate method for each section.

3.15.4 Assuming a message is delivered by media to a specific target audience, does the message have its expected effect? In fact, little or no support has been found for the 'one-step' theory of communication, which suggests that all of those who receive a message will react to it in the same way and that the effects of media are simple and direct. At the same time, other theories jostle for position, and some are briefly summarised below.

3.16 Models of media effects

3.16.1 This social reality model suggests that media do not directly influence our behaviour, but that media messages, however, shape our perception of the world in which we live, and that they also influence the social reality which contains us.

3.16.2 This ability of media to define reality is often highlighted

in the political arena — subtle biasing of news by the use of particular words or pictures and the omission of one event in favour
of another. The 'agenda setting' version of the social reality theory
is another special case generated by the study of media and
politics. Simply stated, the agenda setting argument is that whilst
media do not control our opinions, nor how we think about
issues, they do control the list of issues we think about, the range
of objects about which we have opinions. During a general election
the media do not have a mass effect upon how we vote, but they
dictate the issues that we discuss and in fact set the election
agenda.

3.16.3 The two-step model of media effects is similarly complex
though rather easier to simplify. Studies of rumour, the diffusion
of information, the spread of fashions and so on show that some
people are more active communicators than others. Such people
have been termed 'opinion leaders', they seek out information
and actively pass it along. The theory has it, and there is supporting evidence, that such people are the ones to whom messages
should be transmitted in the first place. The message is legiti-
matised when opinion leaders pass it along to those in their social
network. For example, in a North-East working class estate some
boys achieved status in a physically 'rough' group by becoming
the experts on pop music.[1] In order to do this they spent considerable periods of time listening to pop music on radio and reading the musical weeklies. Nicknames also attest to the importance
of 'two-step' flow amongst young people: 'Prof', 'Mastermind'
and a host of names derived from celebrities — Evilbleeding
Knievel, Barry Sheen, Ché and so on.

3.16.4 The third displacer of a simple cause and effect model
pictures the audience as dynamic. Instead of atoms or pawns
pushed this way and that by media messages, the audience member
is selective, choosing the material which serves felt needs at any
particular time. The researcher's cliché is: We have replaced the
question 'What do media do to young people?' by 'What do people
do with media?'

3.16.5 This 'uses and gratifications' or 'functional' approach has

---

1 Dembo, R and McCron, R — *Social Factors in Media Use* — in Brown, R
(Ed.), op. cit.

been taken up by many researchers. Investigations produce strikingly consistent results in several countries. But again researchers have concentrated on children and adults, ignoring those in between. For example studies of children and media in England and Sweden revealed that television is much less of an escapist medium than many have assumed.[1] Whilst round about 25% of children reported various escapist or mood control uses of television, almost half of the children reported uses of television related to the exploration of reality (learning — or being told about — different places and people, what it's like to be grown up and so on). The most frequently endorsed use of television for these children was as a source of conversation. 30% or more 15 year olds nominated television as being best for: 'letting you know how other people lived', 'finding out about things that happen in different places', 'telling you about things you don't learn in school' and 'giving you things to talk about with friends'.

3.16.6 At nine years of age television seems to be the main source of media based satisfaction, but by fifteen young people are out and about and television is displaced by music and contact with friends. In absolute terms, the young adult is watching, on average, almost twenty hours television each week, but it seems likely that much of this watching is low key and time filling. Another investigation focused on attitudes to television of under 25's and over 25's.[2] Numerous slight variations were revealed, but the most marked difference between the two groups emerged from a question about motives for watching. Of the over 25's, 11% regarded television as a 'way of killing time'; 23% of under 25's selected this answer. This suggests a major difference in overall approach to television.

3.16.7 This brief investigation of existing material, often produced in pursuit of more general or other research, leads us to conclude that not enough is known about the relationship between young people and the media. Indeed, we don't even know with any certainty how young people themselves believe they

---

1 See Brown, R — *Children's Uses of Television* and
  Feilitzen, C von — *The Functions Served by Media*
  both in Brown, R (Ed.) op. cit.
2 BBC Audience Research Department — Difference in Attitudes Between Respondents Aged Over and Under 25 — 1978

respond. A further investigation which reached even that stage would be relevant in improving the effectiveness of the media in its supporting role, particularly to those who have been called disadvantaged.

Part II

The Broadcasters

4 What the broadcasters are doing

4.0 In Part I we looked at what is known about those young people with particular needs in relation to the world of work and what is known about their use of the mass media. In this Part we examine in some detail the present contribution of broadcasting and give some idea of the range of programme provision so that we may see how broadcasters are currently responding to the needs of young people as we, and others, have identified them.

4.1 The nature of public service broadcasting in Britain is encapsulated in the three-fold injunction to 'inform, educate and entertain'. Most, if not all, programmes, whilst falling principally, in one category or another — information, education or entertainment — combine elements of all three. There is, however, a danger that in an investigation of this kind into the needs of young adults, we will tend to focus on the first two elements to the exclusion of the third. We know that young people watch *Top of the Pops* or listen to ILR or BBC Radio 1 simply because they enjoy entertaining output. Such programmes meet a legitimate need and we do not wish to imply in what follows that the only value of such programmes is that they provide a ready-made audience who should then be motivated, stimulated or somehow led on to 'better' things. This Report is not, however, principally about young people's passive entertainment needs as such, but a range of other requirements that may be met by advice, education or training, and the extent to which broadcasting, including entertainment, might help to meet those needs.

4.2 What follows, therefore, is a description of examples of what is, has recently been, or is shortly to be broadcast in direct or indirect response to the needs of young people. Reference to what is on offer demonstrates a wide and varied provision based

61

on extremely good intentions but also suggests gaps in relation to the target group of this Study. It must be stressed that it is not intended to provide an exhaustive list of all current provision. Instead, we have tried to pick out typical and interesting examples which illustrate the range of relevant programming.

4.3 We have followed the broadcasters' practice of dividing output into 'educational' and 'general'. This distinction is in some ways an arbitrary one — many programmes not formally classified as 'educational' are nevertheless educative — and is used by us simply for convenience. However, it is worth noting that a special feature of the 'educational' output for schools and colleges is based on the assumption that the educational function of the programme does not stop short at the end of the broadcast. On the contrary, the programme is in each case intended to be a resource for starting or developing activity, to provoke discussion, invite further exploration of both the realities and opportunities in the outside world and the individual's potential relationship with that world. For the teacher, too, the programme is offered as a resource rather than a substitute teacher, and teachers' booklets contain suggestions for further activity. Often there are also booklets or packs for pupils.

4.4 Output for schools and colleges

Examples of series broadcast during 1977/78 fall broadly into three categories. In all cases these series are part of long-standing commitments to provision in these areas.

4.4.1 *Preparation for employment*

BBC TV continued its provision of two career education series for schools: *Going to Work*, aimed at less academically successful school-leavers, and *A Job Worth Doing?* which is designed for those who will be leaving school with some qualifications. Both of these provided information about particular careers, although in *Going to Work* there is more specific information alternated with programmes which take up an aspect of working life such as relationships with other people at work, work responsibilities, considerations involved in choosing a job, and so on.

BBC Radio for schools has a pattern broadly comparable with that of BBC TV in the area of preparation for working life. *The*

World of Work (1977/78) took up two themes; in the Autumn term topics centred on self-awareness in relation to the world of work, while the Spring programme attempted to answer the question, what does being at work feel like — referring to job interviews, relationships at work, managing an income and so on. Although BBC School Radio's *People at Work* is intended primarily for 13—14 year olds, it could well be used for the older age-groups, and probably is. It deals with the character of different fields of work, such as factory jobs, retailing, self-employment etc.

The BBC's National Regional schools output within Scotland includes one radio series, *Questions of Living*, which is specifically concerned with the situation in that country. It offers school leavers a range of information and ideas about life in the adult world both at home and at work. A BBC Scottish Schools Television series *Living in Scotland* also pursues ideas in relation to social education in the area of job finding and adjusting to life outside school.

It is difficult to summarise the contribution of BBC Local Radio as regions vary widely in the number of education series broadcast, although generally the number is smaller than that on National Radio and provision for the age group is correspondingly sparse and geographically uneven. However, much interesting material is available. To quote some examples: BBC Radio Sheffield's drama series *The Final Year* dealt with the problems of different people approaching the end of their school career. Similarly in the summer 1978, BBC Radio Newcastle offered 'advice and information for young job seekers' plus support material in *A Step in the Right Direction*. Also BBC Radio Birmingham offered *Clock On*, a series designed to introduce 13—14 year olds to industries in the West Midlands; the format of each programme was a visit by a schoolboy and schoolgirl to a local industry to find out about its operation and the training required. BBC Radio Cleveland has had a regular series on careers, consisting each week of a filmed interview by a careers officer and by a school leaver about a young person in a particular job. In addition — BBC Radio Carlisle's workshop project of four half-hour programmes on the theme 'Young people at work and play' is to include interviews with young unemployed people and a host of 'providers' including parents, youth workers, employers, careers officers plus a follow-up group discussion.

There are two major ITV nationally networked series in which working life is dealt with as one among a range of realities in the outside world which the school leaver needs to be prepared to cope with. *Making a Living* (YTV) is intended to provide students with a foretaste of what going to work involves, but is also designed to promote an understanding of the workings of an industrial society, dealing with issues such as the economy and the role of industry. *Work* (ATV) was designed to complement the Schools Council Geography for the Young School Leaver project and looks at employment in a geographical context, examining in a light, humorous style why certain industries are located in certain places, changes in the nature of some jobs such as farming, the effect of industry on the landscape and so on. There have also been ITV schools series which are intended to give the school leaver a picture of the industrial set-up, jobs and training opportunities in their own region; for example, *Its Your Future* (Thames), concentrated on the south-east of England and print back-up was in the form of a pack prepared by the National Extension College, *Work Shop* (Granada) covered the Granada transmission area and ITV's *Leaving School* was for the Yorkshire region.

4.4.2 *Vocational series*

The BBC Education Department also produces television series specifically designed for use by young people studying full or part-time at colleges of further education. Since further education colleges are primarily concerned with vocational courses, this is reflected in the broadcast output which is repeated year by year on a similar basis to the broadcasts for schools. During the period in question, a number of series have been featured, for example, *Engineering Craft Studies*, a series designed to supplement the teaching of the City and Guilds 200 Part 1 courses in basic engineering craft studies; *Tecair Ltd*, a series designed for first and second year technician students; and *The Business World* for students on BEC and SCOTBEC courses.

4.4.3 *Preparation for adult life*

There are other aspects to preparing for adult life apart from choosing jobs and some of these have also been dealt with by educational broadcasts.

ITV's major series in this area, *Starting Out* (ATV), examines the problems of starting work. Among a range of other issues raised are the different kinds of relationships experienced with friends (of either sex), marriage partners, families and the community. This series is unusual in presenting the issues in dramatised serial form — which suggests that broadcasters are looking at the attractiveness of using popular media styles for educational purposes. There is also an ITV education series from Granada called *Politics — What's it all About?* which focuses on helping young adults to see themselves in the context of society. There is discussion of such matters as the roles of elected representatives, the work of trade unions, the way local government operates, the problems faced by members of minority groups such as the handicapped, the tension between the 'good' of the individual and the 'good' of the community. The position of the individual in society is intended to be the key theme of the series and particularly the position of the school leaver and young adult.

BBC Schools Radio's *By the People, for the People* was a one-term series introducing young people to the political structures of this country, with the emphasis on ways in which the public participate in decision-making. The final programme was devoted to viewpoints, including those of young listeners.

ITV's *The English Programme* (Thames), although intended as a resource for English teaching generally, includes a unit of four film documentaries on the experience of 'outsiders' in society, one of which deals with the unemployed.

BBC School TV's *Scene* also raises some controversial social and political issues in either documentary or drama form with the intention of stimulating discussion, and is designed with less academic students in mind.

BBC School Radio's *Enquiry* is an example of a number of series produced by that department in the area of the humanities. In 1977/78 the programmes were about the problems of old and young people, both in the family context and outside it; decision-making in relation to the community, and the broader issues in home and international affairs and their impact on the individual's way of life. Another series with similar aims is *Learning About Life*.

In the area of parenthood there is, for example, an ITV series called *Facts for Life* (Granada). The first four programmes in this series look at conception, pregnancy, childbirth and the first few months of the baby's life; the second four look at some of the responsibilities of parents with small children including health care, the child's needs and so on. The films which are designed to show what actually happens at clinics, in hospital and at home, feature parents and parents-to-be talking about their own experiences.

A number of BBC educational series first broadcast during the evening are repeated during school and college hours. Most relevant are those concerned with active leisure pursuits, particularly sports. Series include *Canoe, Athlete* and *The Craft of the Potter*.

4.5 Educational output – post-school

4.5.1 The series listed above are specifically aimed at the older student and are intended for use in schools or colleges. However, there are also educational series which are designed principally for use by home audiences (though there is also some take-up by institutions) which are potentially helpful to those making the transition from school to work even though they are programmes designed for all adults and not young adults in particular. For example, both BBC and ITV have seen themselves as having a part to play in meeting the needs of adults to acquire basic skills in order to deal with the demands of the current work situation as expressed by BBC's well-established adult literacy series *On the Move* and ITV's numeracy series *Make it Count* (YTV).

4.5.2 Some of the programmes originating from further and adult education departments are also designed for the unemployed. ITV has two series offering practical advice; ATV's *Out of Work?* which was nationally networked and had MSC support, gave advice on how to cope with unemployment, the services available, training opportunities and so on; Ulster's *Want a Job?* on careers in local industry featured a phone-in service provided by careers officers in the Department of Manpower.

4.5.3 A much more ambitious and sophisticated series was mounted by Westward TV called *Just the Job*; the unusual feature was that the MSC and the National Extension College co-operated with Westward to provide a printed pack and a follow-up support network using volunteer counsellors. *Just the Job* type projects are now being discussed in other regions such as Scotland (Scottish TV) and Teeside (Radio Tees). Capital Radio too, (who have considerable experience in co-operating with agencies such as ESD on projects, for example, the ones described above,) have no decided in principle to mount a *Just the Job* style venture.

Cross-media co-operation too is in the air, with Radio Bristol working with an ITV company, HTV, in conjunction with the Careers Service, to find jobs for young people.

4.5.4 Radio Clyde's *Noticeboard* was a phone-in series specifically devoted to the transition from school to work, although not a schools series as such. Over 20 weeks it covered such topics as the Job Extension Scheme, different types of careers programmes for the young unemployed and further education opportunities.

4.5.5 On industrial matters BBC Radio Further Education Department's *Nation at Work* is intended for the working population in general as well as those about to start their working life, and covers such topics as current industrial and commerical issues behind the news, problems at the workplace and the role of particular industries.

4.6 General programmes designed specifically for young people

4.6.1 There are, of course, many general programmes aimed at young people which, although primarily intended as entertainment, have potential for helping them in this transitional period. An obvious example of this kind of output is pop music which is broadcast on many ILR stations and on BBC Radio 1 as well as some television series such as *Top of the Pops*. Pop music output is already, in some cases, being taken as an opportunity to broadcast snippets of information such as job vacancy announcements, mentioned later. This applies chiefly to the output of ILR stations. The advantage of such brief snippets is that they avoid giving the impression to the young listener that he is being 'talked at'. A rather longer 'snippet' is included every Monday between 5.30 and 6.30 pm in BBC Radio 1's Kid Jensen Show. The spot is called the *Kid's Mail Bag* and about twelve listeners' letters are answered on a variety of topics each week; there is an interview with an expert on a related topic. This area of programming is being expanded with the major changes in Radio 1 which started in November 1978.

4.6.2 However, there are programmes involving 'talks' which are aimed at a young audience and try to deal with topics of particular interest to that audience. Several magazine programmes of this kind, such as Radio Victory's *Streetlife*, offer a mixture of music and discussion. BBC Radio 1's *Speakeasy* has had young people in the studio taking part in discussions with experts on a number of moral and political issues. This was replaced by *Talkabout* in November 1978. Radio Thames Valley's *Drive Time* goes out in the 'tea-time' period and features lighter material.

4.6.3 Similar programmes are also beginning to appear on television. *Pauline's People* (Thames) is a chat-show with a studio audience and a young presenter in which topics of interest to young people are looked at in a light-hearted way, using a mixture of studio interviews and film interspersed with music; also HTV West's *Breaktime*, described as 'essentially a making and doing magazine for teenagers'.

4.6.4 On BBC TV there has so far been only one major effort recently to design a television series for this age group, bringing together various items ranging from rock music to a discussion of political issues. This was *Something Else*, produced by the Community Programmes Unit and broadcast in March 1978. This evolved as a result, firstly, of a survey of young people carried out by the Unit, and secondly, from a small group of young people brought together on the basis of this survey in order to design the content of the programme. The aim was to attempt to create something which the majority of young people would recognise as being for and about them.

4.6.5 The most sustained Features/Current Affairs series for this age group is LWT's *London Weekend Show*. Recently it devoted a programme to youth unemployment but has covered many other topics such as punk music, black Londoners, etc. Its mixture of interviews, vox pop, popular presenter and concentration on themes of direct interest to young people, give it a greater potential for reaching the target than the regular features programmes on television.

4.6.6 As far as news and current affairs programmes are concerned, BBC 1's *Nationwide* is the one BBC television offering which makes a particular effort to appeal to young people while remaining essentially a programme for all ages. This programme is broadcast on BBC 1 at 5.55 — 6.20 pm Monday to Friday, the time young people in the IFF study particularly favoured. Items which are seen to be of particular concern to this age group are included on an occasional basis, and in addition, special features aimed at the young are built on a regular basis, such as 'Young Nation 1977' and 'Lifelines'. These include items about employment and unemployment, parental conflict, as well as lighter aspects of youth culture.

4.6.7 On ITV, in addition to *The London Weekend Show*, there is Granada's *What's New*, which is a news programme specifically for teenagers. However, this series is for local transmission only.

4.6.8 Of news and current affairs items on radio, the only offering designed primarily for young people is *Newsbeat* on BBC Radio 1. *Newsbeat* is a fifteen minute programme of news and current affairs broadcast at 12.30 pm and 5.30 pm each weekday, and unlike *Nationwide* is designed in style and content more for the younger listeners who make up a large proportion of its audience. As a consequence it regularly features items of news or stories which are of particular relevance to the themes being examined by this Study.

4.6.9 Another emerging type of programme is described as 'Junior Access', in which a number of under 20's are invited into a studio to make programmes, not as representatives of an organisation but as members of a generation speaking directly to fellow members. In addition to *Something Else*, mentioned earlier, a pioneering project of this kind was ITV's *You Can Make It* (Tyne Tees) in which 8–18 year olds were given the opportunity to make their own films. Another new series is scheduled for 1978/79.

4.6.10 *Straight Down the Line* was a four programme phone-in series on BBC Radio 4 offering an opportunity for young people to phone in with their ideas on a number of themes. This format is being taken up on Radio 1 from November 1978. Capital Radio is planning a one-off programme called *Speak for Yourself* in which, as the title implies, young people in the studio exchange views on topics of particular interest to them arising out of the Youth Charter 2000 Conference.

4.7 **Other relevant 'general' output**

It is not sufficient in this review to consider only those series produced specifically for young people either by the education departments or other parts of the broadcasting organisations. Although comprehensive in their scope, the broadcasts to schools and colleges must, by their very nature, have only a limited impact on young people as a whole. The other programmes or items for young people described in the previous section are not at all numerous. The impact of general broadcasting output as a whole must obviously be considered, whether or not it is designed primarily for the young. This is where the major resources of staff and money are to be found, these are the programmes transmitted at 'peak' hours and this is naturally where the largest audiences are — and that means the largest audiences of young adults too. This is where everyone gets from the media most of their information about the world in which they move.

4.7.1 In that context there is scarcely a station or channel which has not covered the problems of the unemployed or other serious social, economic or political issues, at one time or another, at least in documentaries — whether one-off, such as the 'Unemployment — Public Enemy No. 1' programme in BBC TV's *Man Alive*, or a series, such as ATV's *Great Expectations* which follows a group of school leavers through their last year at school and first year in the world of work. Then there are the current affairs series such as *Weekend World* (LWT), *World in Action* (Granada) and *Panorama* (BBC) which deal with such issues as a matter of course.

4.7.2 Many programmes have been designed to give practical information and help to the unemployed in general. ATV's *Jobline* was an example of a type of locally orientated programme giving advice on how to set about finding a job. Such programming is becoming more common, particularly on local radio, and clearly has special relevance to the school leaver. BBC Radio Blackburn's *Workwise* gives advice on how to go about getting a job; it was a 13 week series of 15 minute programmes broadcast in 1977. Radio Orwell's *My Job* series featured people in different jobs telling about their work, the skills required and so on. On BBC's national radio there is the World of Work item in *You and Yours* (BBC Radio 4) on Mondays at lunchtime in which details of employment vacancies and career opportunities are given. Metro's

Gateway gives information for those 'with time on their hands' about training schemes, voluntary and social work.

4.7.3 Stations operating a regular 30 second or one minute notice-board of local vacancies are too numerous to mention. Typically the announcements are made at the same point each hour and the vacancies advertised are provided by the local job centre or employment services. Some stations, such as Piccadilly, also trail a number for employers to ring in with vacancies. Radio Trent report that in one day they received information on 33 vacancies from employers. Orwell and similar stations have experienced a considerable response to trailing off-air phone-in services offered by other agencies, whether they are employment services as already described or voluntary agencies offering a range of counselling and other help.

4.7.4 All local stations have their own magazine programmes which, while admittedly watched mainly by an older audience, do go on the air usually in the early evening when young people are more likely to be at home, and do offer an opportunity for items of concern to that group. *About Anglia* (Anglia) for instance, recently devoted a programme to job information, calling it *Job Shop*. Some stations have had one-off 'job weeks' in which the drive to obtain and fill job vacancies has been made a feature throughout the week and a good example is BRMB's July 1977 *Job Week* mounted in conjunction with the then ESA. Information on career opportunities, both in training and employment, was broadcast; a number of careers experts were interviewed in the studio; and an enquiry centre set up at Birmingham Council House staffed by trained counsellors, with a special switchboard manned 12 hours a day. There are no figures available for the response but when Radio Trent ran a similar *Job Week*, 110 of the 650 calls received were from people under 18. Of course the phone-in is well established in local radio programming as a source of information, advice and help with personal problems, but is now being extended into areas like consumer and legal advice, with the co-operation of outside agencies. Specifically on employment, Radio Leicester's *Crosstalk* regularly features Department of Employment advice. Equally a number of local community service programmes whether networked like Granada's *Reports Action* or local like Thames' *Help*! have included information on job opportunities. *Help!* in fact has a weekly employment slot covering topics such as employment, medical advisory and occupational guidance services. Radio Beacon offers *Topic*, a current affairs and news magazine which goes out during the early evening each day for two hours. It concentrates mainly on news, both world and local, and leisure topics with a local slant. However in summer 1977 Job Centre people came into the studio to talk about the role of the Job Centre, how to go about getting a job, and what sort of vacancies were available.

4.8 Programming for those with young adults in their care

4.8.1 Finally some mention should be made of output aimed at helping parents and teachers of young adults, as well as for others having responsibilities for those entering the world of work. In fact there is little being done in this area and what exists has come only from educational broadcasting. Both BBC and IBA have a permanent commitment to offer parent education series and in-service series for teachers. Currently for parents there is *Parents and School* on BBC TV and *Parents Day* (Granada) on ITV, although both of these are about school-age children generally, they do touch on the particular needs of adolescents and school leavers. For example, one programme of the *Parents and School* series considered the relationship of school and industry.

4.8.2 For other 'providers' there is *The School Year* on BBC Radio 3 in 1977/78 which covers personal and social developments from the age of 5 to 16. In 1978/9 however, BBC is scheduling two series on television; *Taste of Work* which will help inform providers of both jobs and training of the range of opportunities now available to the young unemployed and *Working with Young People*, also designed for those working with young people, particularly on schemes for the young unemployed, featuring filmed case studies which indicate good practice.

Caveat

This Chapter has given an indication of the range of programme output which is relevant to the purposes of this Study. It looks impressive at first glance but is in some ways misleading. A totally different impression of current provision will be gained by a flick through any issue of the *TV Times* or *Radio Times*. Programmes for young people, particularly if one excludes school broadcasting, far from being plentiful are, in fact, relatively hard to find. In the next Chapter there is an assessment of the ways in which the full impact of the broadcasting provision which does exist is lost.

5 The gap between provision and need

5.0 The last Chapter looked at the range of broadcasts designed for young people or likely to be of direct interest to them, or to those adults with direct responsibility for young people. The number and scope of these programmes, particularly bearing in mind that it is not an exhaustive list, seems impressive and consequently broadcasters might be forgiven for believing that they were contributing a great deal. This Chapter draws attention to those factors which lessen the impact of this apparently generous provision.

5.1 Some aspects of this gap between provision and need may be inherent in the nature of broadcasting. For example, on the one hand broadcasting is a *mass* medium but, on the other hand, the needs of the viewer or listener may require *individual* attention. We believe that broadcasters themselves can do much, given the will, to minimise this gap.

5.2 Educational broadcasting for schools and colleges

5.2.1 There are, of course, many schools broadcasts on radio and television about young people's transition from school to adult life, both in terms of career and job choice and, more generally, in terms of the individual's personal social development towards adult life. This educational broadcasting, as we remarked earlier, is frequently intended to be used within an institutional context and it is the teacher or tutor who attempts to maximise its impact in line with certain pre-determined curricular objectives. Such schools provision will thus be related to the particular needs of a given class, and to the needs of the individuals in that class. Much care is taken in the devising of support material, such as booklets for teachers and pupils, and in evaluating the response of teachers to the broadcast series. What is more, there is a ready concern on the part of the educational staff within the broadcasting organisations to ensure that the priorities of teachers and pupils in schools are reflected in what is being planned for future transmission.

5.2.2 That said, however successful the impact of schools broadcasting is, it is less than it might be for several reasons. First, only a proportion of the age group which we are here concerned with is actually in schools or colleges. Most young people after the age of sixteen are in full-time work and not available to view or listen during the working day. Secondly, only a minority of secondary schools make regular use of such series. The BBC's *Going To Work*, itself the most widely used series by secondary schools, is taken by only just over one third of these schools in any year. Thirdly, the impact of the programmes themselves varies greatly from school to school and from class to class. Evidence from visits by broadcasting staff and from independent sources (for example, the Hayter Report on *Using Broadcasts in Schools*) suggests that there is a wide variation in the teachers' abilities to exploit the broadcast material effectively. Perhaps most fundamentally, many young people who will face the most profound problems when they leave school have already, by senior secondary stage, rejected all aspects of the school provision of help and advice. This is likely to include schools broadcasting along with everything else.

5.3 Educational output — post-school

5.3.1 Broadcasting for schools, aiming as it does to meet the continuing needs of young people, attempts to offer over the years a continuous flow of broadcast material on the major themes related to the needs of young people facing the move out of school and into the wider world. In relation to the post-school output, however, the broadcasters are in a difficult position, given, particularly in ITV's present case, the constraints of air time. The need to provide educational series for those who have left school — across an almost limitless range of adult needs and interests — tends to mean that continuity of provision in any but a general sense is difficult to maintain. Thus, faced with requests to involve themselves in broadcast contributions throughout the spectrum of adult and continuing education, the broadcasters have inevitably seen it as their duty to be involved only temporarily in any one area. In certain cases, for example with the BBC's involvement on Adult Literacy, this commitment may be for three or more years, or in the case of foreign language courses there may be a 'rolling' commitment to provide say, beginners courses once every three years. But the needs of young people continue year in and year out and require a response which this form of broadcasting, for quite valid reasons, may not be able or may not wish to guarantee.

5.3.2 Another limitation which affects the impact of educational broadcasting is that, for the most part, series produced by education departments have tended to get scheduled at out of the way times when only a relatively small number of people, young or old, are viewing — late at night or early on Sunday mornings, for example. Alternatively, if the hours are good the less popular channels are selected. However much thought may have gone into devising such programmes they are likely to have only little impact as a result. For instance, although this has just changed, BBC Further Education Radio has had its main outlet on Radio 3 through the week. This is obviously not the best location to reach the main mass of young people (or their parents) — popular times and channels are essential, at least for some of the time.

5.4 'General' output for young people

5.4.1 Other than school and college broadcasting, young people within the age group 14—21 have few special television programmes. Peter Fiddick, in an article in *The Listener* in April 1978, summed up this situation by saying that broadcasting for young adults was like a fishing net where the holes were more significant than the net. The output of Children's Programmes Departments, for example, is usually for a younger age group, although there are certainly some pioneering ventures at the lower end of the Study age-band. *Pauline's People* (Thames) illustrates one of the approaches that seeks to mix an entertaining format with serious discussion topics for young people. There are other examples of programmes specifically for young adults including Tyne Tees' *You Can Make It*, Granada's *What's New*, a news programme for teenagers and *The London Weekend Show* (LWT) and they go some way towards meeting the needs of young people as we here define them, although only within specific local transmission areas. There is no pattern of local provision across the country as a whole.

5.4.2 Radio provision, both nationally and locally, is also inadequate. There seems to be a belief that young people are willing to listen to nothing other than pop music in its various forms. Various initiatives have been taken at a local and national level, but far more thought needs to be given, particularly on BBC Radio 1, to ways in which serious output might be integrated into the overall popular output.

5.4.3 Moreover, the fact that a given programme on radio or television meets a need does not guarantee its continuing existence in the schedules. For example, a single trial programme *Something Else* conceived by the BBC's Community Programmes Unit and run by and for young people was generally very warmly received when it was transmitted early in 1978. (It was also very well received by young people during the IFF Study.) It was expected that this idea would be extended into a continuing series but in the event presumably its, and young people's, claim to air time proved to be less important than more conventional programming for other groups.

5.4.4 Certainly *Something Else* was an attempt to experiment with regard to content and indeed to ask young people themselves what they wanted. The content of such programmes could well be developed not only to include youth topics — fashion, examinations, skate-boarding, 'punk' or whatever else is 'popular' — but more importantly to see and help explain the world as young people see it and live in it.

5.4.5 Over and over again people have said that broadcasting can change attitudes — or reinforce existing stereotypes. If this is so, broadcasters should recognise their responsibilities in relation to young people. The point was frequently made to us that broadcasting, when it features young people, does so in caricatures, brainy 'whizz kids' or wild tearaways. In particular it tends to reinforce the traditional view of the role of girls. 'Hands that do dishes . . .' are invariably female. This type of stereotyping affects young people and adults alike and certainly affects the potential value of broadcast provision.

5.5 General programmes for 'adult' groups, parents, professional workers

5.5.1 The range of topics dealt with in general programmes is very wide; inevitably there are some programmes of value to those who have young people in their care. ATV's recent series of documentaries *Great Expectations* is perhaps the best recent example of a series that heightened public awareness and understanding of the various issues involved in a young person's transition from school to work. Similarly, documentaries about unemployment, such as the BBC's *Unemployment — Public Enemy No. 1*, do much to help adults understand the changing world in which their children are growing up.

5.5.2 It is quite possible that a few 'ordinary' young people, either employed or unemployed, seen on television discussing their particular problems might do quite a bit to foster adults' understanding of the needs and problems of youth. A documentary about what it is like to be young and unemployed seen from the viewpoint of that young person could well create a climate of sympathy and a potential focus in relation to unemployment as *Cathy Come Home* did for homelessness.

5.5.3 Sadly, even if a documentary of this sort is produced there is rarely machinery for following it up, for further discussion by parents, youth workers and so on. Such people don't receive any significant advance warning that the programme is on — a week's notice is not long enough. Educational broadcasts, of course, do offer longer notice but with one or two exceptions the in-service needs of professional youth workers, teachers, careers officers, or indeed parents, have not been sufficiently recognised, and certainly not when considering the potentially valuable resource for in-service work that general programming undoubtedly is.

Two other general points about broadcasting for young adult groups, and their 'mentors', were made by those consulted. Although they have been touched on already they are worth looking at in some detail in our attempt to look at the gap that exists between broadcast provision and need.

5.6 Style

5.6.1 Young people in the IFF discussion groups clearly felt more attention should be paid to style — the style of programmes was as important as an appreciation of suitable content. They expressed general agreement that programmes *for* young people should be presented *by* young people though perhaps not, they said, by people who were so young that they lacked the necessary competence and air of authority. Certainly no one over forty would be suitable, even thirty-five would be 'pushing it'. Adult groups too saw the presenter as being of crucial importance in the overall style of the programme.

5.6.2 Both young people and adults referred to the importance of a popular, even 'pop' format. Some employers, the younger ones, interviewed by IFF also recognised the potentially key role of pop music and the need to intersperse any factual content with it. This, it was thought, was epitomised by the output of what many saw as one of the best independent local radio stations, Capital Radio.

> "I think that is because it is a mainly pop station and when they have their programme on Sunday and they talk about the 'O' levels or they have their 'phone-ins' they do bursts of pop music in between, so it holds their interest, and basically that is all the young people are interested in, that's pop music."
>
> (London employer)

5.6.3 Studio discussions in particular were considered to be boring and an exchange about the merits of *The London Weekend Show* (LWT), a programme which seemed to the London young people interviewed to have most of the required ingredients for a young adults' programme, reveals this anti-studio discussion bias:

> "It isn't one that seems boring" (ie *London Weekend Show*)
> "What seems boring to you?"
> "People sitting there yak-yak round a table"
> "Panorama."

5.6.4 There was criticism, particularly by these young people, of much of schools broadcasting which was felt, in many cases unfairly, to be too didactic. Many adult groups argued that the style of presentation needed to be as different as possible from that experienced through teachers at school even though the young people would probably watch the programme in school. Some employers suggested a documentary technique, for example the progress of young people leaving school and starting work might be followed. Others felt that the 'soap opera' approach was appealing. A point of style that was regularly mentioned was the need for humour; *Fawlty Towers*, Kenny Everett's television and radio shows and *Monty Python* were all obviously highly popular and acceptable to the age group.

5.6.5 In short, it was felt that if the style was right television and radio could help young people in a way that other agencies couldn't. The following comment from a London employer is typical and gives support to the views of the young people.

> "Job Centres and Careers Officers try, but they still think it's the school and it's a school teacher and the natural thing is to dislike your school teacher. Maybe — you know, it needs a different type of person."

However, a point frequently made by adults and young people alike was that the potential that broadcasting had to help young people was not being realised.

5.7 Scheduling

5.7.1 The young people also felt that if programming of the sort they wanted were to be developed, the traditional schools broadcasting slots would be no use. They would, they argued, watch television if it met their needs and if programmes were transmitted at 'their time'. Tea-time transmissions were seen as the most appropriate slot, around 5–7 pm. Weekend mornings, though needless to say not too early, were also mentioned. The success of Westward Television's *Just the Job*, transmitted at 5.15 pm, indicates that there might be some truth in this — certainly the series held and increased its audience. Adults were even more critical of the broadcasters' present scheduling arrangements but agreed that specific minority programming (*eg* in-service work for teachers,) might legitimately be transmitted in non-peak hours. What seemed less legitimate was the notion of educational 'ghetto hours', at least as far as the popular channels were concerned, regardless of the target audience.

5.7.2 Appropriate scheduling of radio items for young people is less restricted not only because of the near universal ownership of transistor radios, but also because the output is more flexible and easily allows a sequence of short inserts into an existing programme — an approach, some argue, that is particularly suitable for young adults.

*   *   *   *   *

5.8 We said earlier that broadcasting is first and foremost a *mass* medium — that is true, of course, even in its local or regional forms. Significantly, many people stressed the importance of the local dimension in programming. In terms of schools broadcasting, the BBC's National Regions do make a significant provision but ITV and local radio's provision clearly have the greatest potential here. So far the local educational dimension has not been sufficiently exploited in relation to young people's needs. Some ITV Companies and the BBC's national regions have been even slower to develop general programmes for young people. That said, young people's 'needs' for information for example may well be local, but their 'wants', the things and people with which they identify, may be far from local. Network provision is thus vital too and it may be that the recipe for programming outlined elsewhere in this Report, linked to print and other support activities, may help to close the gap between the intention of broadcasts and the needs of young people.

5.9 We mentioned earlier that the extensive sample of broadcast provision given in Chapter 4 looks rather less impressive when one considers what programmes might actually be available to a given young person, on a given day, in say, Exeter, Glasgow or Belfast. It obviously is not enough surely to list all of the titles or even quantify them in terms of, for example, money spent or air time occupied. Schools and colleges broadcasting makes a contribution to meeting young people's needs, but broadcasters should not see this as their only or even major response, relevant to this Study. General output so often misses the opportunity to use, to the greatest effect, its ability to reach out to young people. This is chiefly due to the broadcasters' unwillingness to recognise that young people represent a separate section of the listening and viewing public with unique needs which, though they overlap with the needs of a general adult audience, also possess dimensions which are exclusive to young people and which are important enough to be reflected in programme output.

5.10 However sincere the programmers' intentions, there is in practice we feel a major gap between provision and need. What the broadcasters might do about this is the subject of the next Chapter.

6 What else can broadcasting do?

6.0 Too great a distinction between 'educational' programmes and 'general' programmes alluded to in the last Chapter, particularly that part of general output that is educative in intent, may actually be unhelpful as far as young people are concerned. Indeed, a recent IBA Working Party on the relationship between adult education and general output programming, though not principally concerned with the needs of people in the 14–21 age group, referred to this distinction between educative and educational as reinforcing

> "lines of demarcation derived from more conventional institutional patterns of teaching than from the range of learning possibilities inherent in home viewing, and in the fullest exploitation of the mass media."

6.1 This Study is concerned, moreover, not only with young people viewing in schools and colleges, but also with this 'range of learning possibilities' — non-traditional as well as established and conventional, and with the 'fullest exploitation' of the mass media referred to above, in this case principally for the benefit of young people. Thus we are in no doubt that although educational broadcasting is effective with certain sections of the age group (and would be more so if not limited by budget and, even more, by time slot), general programmes have a crucial role to play in giving information and help to those young people — the majority — who leave school at the first opportunity and hope never to grace an educational institution again; these same people spend considerable amounts of time watching television and, even more, listening to the radio.

6.2 Strengths of the media

General observation, and some of the enquiries initiated by this project, have suggested that the particular strengths of the media, especially broadcasting, include their ability to:-

—   reach those who shy away from statutory or voluntary agencies from lack of interest, knowledge or confidence;

—   offer a wide range of information in an easily digestible and succinct manner, sometimes simultaneously with a variety of people including the young, their teachers and their parents;

—   offer insights into the world outside the school, home or a particular work environment, which are not easily available to the individual even when he or she has an interest in acquiring them;

—   offer an anonymity often welcomed by those who have or feel they have already been labelled enough by established society;

—   endow, for a variety of reasons including its inevitable preoccupation with the distinguished, the famous or the plain notorious, with glamour and sense of style and occasion, however essentially mundane or low-key the activities — *eg* the interest and effectiveness of *Police Call* or *Police Five* compared with notices outside police stations. This ability to enhance indirectly the status of people or activities helps to raise the self-esteem of disadvantaged groups merely by its recognition of their problems. The role of *On The Move* within the Adult Literacy campaign was crucial, for example, in motivating and stimulating those who might have been alienated by, or ill-disposed to, standard exhortations;

—   teach. There is now some evidence which suggests that in certain circumstances the media can teach certain basic skills — literacy, numeracy, social and survival skills, and including techniques related to anything from claiming benefit to personal health. The preliminary conclusions of a current IBA Fellowship by David Stringer focusing on YTV's numeracy series *Make It Count*, indicate, albeit tentatively, the potential of broadcast teaching methods in basic education;

change attitudes. Very importantly, there is also considerable support for the idea that the media can effectively change attitudes and influence opinion at all levels of society and that this ability should be used constructively in support of sections of society currently at risk. Indeed, these abilities of broadcasting within the context of this Study are probably particularly important as far as the young unemployed, the 'careerless' or those having difficulty, in some way or another, with the transition from school to work are concerned.

6.3 Role of non-broadcasting media

The investigation initiated by this Study into young people's behaviour in regard to the media has clearly indicated the importance of media other than broadcasting. Within the short timespan of this Study it has not been possible to consider these media, whether mass circulation teenage magazines or small local examples of the 'alternative press' in their own right. Where we have considered print media, this has been in relation to its potential role as a partner with broadcasting. Of particular importance, however, is the evidence (described more fully in Chapter 3) that young adults, relative to other age groups, are frequent readers of national newspapers, weekly magazines, comics and, in all probability, posters, leaflets and the 'alternative press' generally. Moreover, the recent evidence of the 'Douglas' study[1] that the reading ability of the educationally unqualified actually increases after they have left school, may indicate that the printed word particularly in its 'popular' forms is a more effective way of reaching young people than we had once believed — perhaps especially once the initial interest has been aroused by broadcasting. Collaborative ventures between broadcasting and some of these popular forms of print might be particularly interesting. There is clearly a need to explore this area in more detail.

6.4 Role of broadcast media

Thus, it is the belief of the Study team that, given the back-

---

1 J.W.B. Douglas and Nicola Cherry — *Does Sex Make Any Difference?* *Times Educational Supplement* — 9th December 1977

ground outlined above, the answer to the question of what else the media can do must fall in two key areas.

6.4.1 First, it may be necessary to develop new strands of broadcasting either for a specifically educational or a more popular purpose. There is simply not enough programming for young people.

6.4.2 Secondly, methods of exploitation and linkage of existing programmes or new programmes must be developed which might enable the needs of young people to be met more effectively.

Clearly the development of such strategies must involve partnerships with relevant agencies, outside broadcasting, which are capable of following up the initial interest stimulated by the programmes.

6.5 Exploitation

A belief in the use of broadcast material as part of a larger package is not, of course, new. Various models have been developed, for example – and most spectacularly – the Open University. The broadcast element in this instance, however, is part of a tailormade multi-media package – it does not therefore illustrate the potential gain that might be achieved from exploiting material not designed specifically for an educational purpose. Indeed this question of whether and how partnerships might be built around general output material as opposed to specific planned educational broadcasts, and for the less academically inclined at that, has only just recently been seriously discussed. Yet, if young people have rejected conventional institutional patterns of teaching – and there is no doubt that many have – then it is crucial that a new range of learning opportunities should be made available. The broadcasting organisations are already aware of the potential in this area – both the IBA's 16–19 Working Party and the BBC's 15–19 Working Party referred to the potential of greater exploitation of general programming. This is not the place to explore such possibilities in detail, but during the Study various models of linkage between broadcasting and other media and ways of exploiting existing broadcast provision have been suggested. It may be worth recording some of these suggestions.

6.5.1 The 'phone-in' is now widely accepted as a normal part of broadcasting. At its simplest level, the phone-in element can provide a means of identification with a programme as a result of hearing 'real' people putting their points of view. Information given or received in this way may be more acceptable to young people. Perhaps of more fundamental importance is the use of the telephone as a simple device for giving the audience access (after the broadcast has ended) to detailed information which the broadcasts have stimulated them to want. The BBC does this as part of its Adult Literacy project, enabling people to telephone and ask for help in learning to read or write, or to offer help as a tutor. Capital Radio in its *Helpline* provides a service of advice off-air as well as a service on-air. The local radio phone-ins following BBC 2's *Brass Tacks*, although not, of course, catering principally for young people, illustrate another possible line of development. Such linkage following a tea-time magazine programme on topics specifically related to young people could be very effective. Of course, it could be argued, doubtless with some justification, that the most disadvantaged young people are not able to use the phone without help. However, it is important also to remember that many, perhaps most, including more articulate young people, who may or may not also be disadvantaged in some measure, meet problems whilst entering and after entering the labour market.

6.5.2 During the Study our attention has frequently been drawn to the importance of 'serious programming', *eg* documentaries. Some people regretted that supporting supplementary print material is rarely offered. In fact, although such programmes are little watched by young people, they are watched by adults who have young people in their care. Thus, if ATV's recent *Great Expectations* had announced "If you want more information, contact . . ." many parents or professional groups might well have responded. (The programmes might also have been welcomed as in-service training exercises with, say, Careers Officers, had they been available in, for example, cassette form.) Interestingly enough, teachers concerned about the development of economic and political literacy have suggested a print supplement to programmes dealing with political and economic matters. The Head Teacher of Collins Dean Grammar School in Bolton, for example, thought that such supplements would be of much more value than 'straight' educational broadcasts about political and economic subjects. Such notes would be a valuable resource within the school or college, particularly if printed cheaply on duplicated sheets. Moreover, it would not be necessary to infringe copyright if material was viewed at home for subsequent discussion at school or college.

6.5.3 'Popular programmes' could also be exploited more effectively. It is significant that the DJ who brightly asks someone who phones in,
"What do you do . . .?" and is told
"I can't get a job," is more likely to utter a well intentioned
"Yeah, there's a lot of it around" rather than to issue an invitation to all those who are listening and who might be similarly placed to phone or write for information about benefits, training schemes, further education opportunities and so on. (An actual case reported to us during the Study.)

6.5.4 Another topic of relevance in any consideration of the development of popular programming is (with or without liaison with other agencies) the potential of Central Office of Information (COI) 'fillers' when placed next to, or in the advertisement breaks during those popular programmes which attract a large youth audience. Our research, for example, has drawn attention to the importance of series such as *Match of the Day* (boys) or *Crossroads* (girls). COI fillers about YOP or further education opportunities placed next to these programmes could be very effective. The potential of such modest 'filler' additions should not be minimised. For example, when STV started showing the COI's Adult Literacy campaign filler, there was a most dramatic increase in the number of people who came forward. It is reasonable to assume that similar advertisements specifically designed to give young people greater access to education or training opportunities would, if placed in or near 'their' programmes, make a substantial contribution towards raising the level of young people's consciousness and indeed, the consciousness of their parents.

6.6 Administrative implications

Although broadcasters could implement some of the above possibilities without too much difficulty, many extensions of broadcast activity require more than administrative goodwill. They require far more liaison and co-operation with a range of agencies outside broadcasting than is normally possible. Such 'partnerships', whether with agencies such as the Manpower Services Commission, the Department of Education and Science, the TUC, the CBI, popular newspapers and magazines, or agencies such as the National Youth Bureau, may require a new administrative structure if they are to be organised and developed on anything other than an 'ad hoc' basis. Some of this additional administrative effort might quite properly fall to the broadcasting organisations, but in most cases this would seem to be inappropriate. We are forced to conclude that if broadcasters are to respond to the needs of young people, or any other group, then perhaps mechanisms must be developed which enable them to do so without putting an intolerable administrative strain on their own organisations. We make a number of recommendations in Chapter 8.

6.7 Broadcasting and participation

6.7.1 In many ways, therefore, this Study is concerned with new but increasingly common and accepted notions of what broadcasting is all about. If this is an age of participation and if broadcasters are to be nowadays more often involved in a direct dialogue with the community, at local, regional and national level than has previously been the case, then this must be reflected in the opportunities broadcasting affords young people and older groups too. It is now no longer accurate to describe broadcasting as solely a one-way medium of communication. The comment made by Liebje Hoekendijk, the Dutch pioneer of social action television, "There's only one thing wrong with television, it always has the last word — 'Goodnight'," is certainly less true than it was — but for young people it still remains too true.

6.7.2 Various interesting developments have already occurred. On a modest level, direct dialogue between broadcasters and the general public now might involve the familiar debate with a studio audience or a phone-in programme as outlined above. In addition, though still in limited measure, minority groups increasingly seek to gain access to broadcasting resources in order to put their case. On a more ambitious level there has been the development of the 'social action' programmes referred to above which have the specific purpose of soliciting response from their audience to participate in socially useful activities. The nature of this response necessitates detailed co-operative planning between the broadcasters and the social agencies concerned.

Still greater collaboration centres around Westward TV's *Just the Job* which enlists the active participation of both those in need of help and those prepared to give it on a local basis. Similar active co-operation will be necessary in the related urban project, based on STV, currently being planned and on similar local radio models. Such projects required a type of collaboration, a dimension that is new to broadcasting, described by this Study as 'partnership'. The National Extension College has been a very active partner in such activities at both a national and a local level as have other agencies, for example, Community Service Volunteers, who work closely with Thames TV's *Help* series and Granada's networked series *Reports Action*. The BBC's involvement in the Adult Literacy campaign or, at a local radio level, the development in 1977 of the *Child Care Switchboard* involving a number of BBC Local Radio Stations, are other recent examples of the ability of broadcasting to become one part of a network though which those who are seeking help are put into contact with volunteers and/or organisations prepared to offer it.

6.7.3 The thread running through activities of these kinds is the idea of offering some help or support to groups with difficulties. The very success of the media's ability to arouse the interest of those in need and those who can give help does, of course, depend on the broadcasters' ability to respond effectively. Normally, broadcasting organisations are not organised, staffed or financed to provide elaborate back up and reinforcement services and, many broadcasters would add, nor should they be. All of which strengthens both the broadcasters' need to co-operate with other agencies which might provide these services and the need to develop schemes which will be mutually acceptable. Co-operative arrangements can be long or short term, simple or elaborate, but they need to be accepted as proper partnerships which do not exploit the difficulties or needs of one sector in order to bolster the other's empire. In short, partnerships involve both mutual responsibilities and a potential for action. By working in partnerships broadcasters can not only reach the target group but also help, through other agencies, once that contact has been made.

6.8 **Future developments**

The strategies of exploitation, linkage and partnership outlined **above** are all in the realm of the present or the immediate future.

Other changes and possibilities are more speculative but must be borne in mind by those who seek to examine broadcasting's future contribution to young people.

6.8.1 The project officers, for example, have been impressed by the range of *technical developments* that are beginning to make themselves felt. For example, although television and radio broadcasting are already, and hopefully will increasingly be, major components in systems providing for the education and training needs of young people, other forms of audio-visual media will have an increasingly important part to play in the relatively near future. Teletext and Prestel (previously called Viewdata) are two such developments. The advantages of having such systems closely linked to broadcasting is obvious. Factual information relating to programme items can be displayed and cross-referred. In the context of this Study information might relate to availability of jobs, education and training courses, sources of careers advice, benefits available to the unemployed etc. Such links need not be limited to education programmes but can also relate, for example, to current affairs and documentaries. One example of this has already occurred; Oracle (IBA's teletext system) linked with Capital Radio (one of London's ILR stations) provided a regularly updated list of job vacancies.

Whether or not a recent Open University report on *Alternative Media Technologies* is correct when it forecasts that within ten years most British homes will have television sets modified to receive these information systems, there is no doubt that an awareness of these systems should be in the forefront of the minds of those developing media strategies for young people.

6.8.2 Much attention has also been paid to the growing market for *audio and video cassettes*. Video discs have also been mentioned. It has been suggested that some transmissions could be replaced by a cassette distribution service or at least transmission, for recording, at unsocial hours. Our view is that cassette developments will *not* replace the need for transmission and the view is accepted that, at best, education through cassettes will be like education through books — restricted in access. On the other hand, the use of cassettes to supplement existing provision and lead towards the development of resource banks is a totally different matter and might actually lead to more groups of people gaining access to education and training, or simply being helped.

The distribution by Capital Radio of cassettes of the Youth Charter 2000 Conference to youth clubs, schools and other organisations for further discussion may well point the way towards some interesting future initiatives.

6.8.3 At the time of writing, the Government's White Paper on the future of broadcasting has only recently been published. One of its major proposals is for setting up an Open Broadcasting Authority (OBA) which would be responsible for output on the fourth television network. This network would draw on a variety of sources for its broadcasts (including the existing programme-makers in the BBC and ITV companies,) in order to provide an output which caters particularly for the needs of minority groups in the community. We imagine that the claims of young people would at least be favourably considered by an OBA, or any other structure, for example an ITV2. Indeed, the Annan Report which led to the White Paper specifically said,

> "We should like to single out the needs of those in the 16—19 age group who are not taking a course of higher education or training and who need to be helped with the choice of their careers; the likelihood of increased re-training and in-service courses; the needs of those for whom school has not provided the basic skills of literacy and numeracy . . ."

6.9 Regardless of the results of subsequent Parliamentary discussions about the OBA, broadcasters already have the wherewithal to do more for young adults. They are free to extend and develop their provision and to co-operate with those external agencies who work with and for young people at grass roots or national level. New technological developments will create fresh opportunities but the future of broadcasting in relation to young adults and those who have young adults in their care may depend on present will as much as future Governmental policy. Thus, the next Chapters contains our final conclusions and recommendations and will look at what should be done by broadcasters now, on their own and, more importantly, with others, regardless of any significant change in broadcasting policy.

Part III

Conclusions and Recommendations

7 Conclusions

7.0 In this Report we have attempted to outline some of the needs of young people and to explore what broadcasting is doing and also might do. From time to time we have referred to the economic context within which this Study is set and this Chapter of conclusions needs to be read with an awareness of the basic economic imperatives. We are moving into a phase in our history in which changes in technology will affect young people more directly than any other group in the work force. The situation is one which is not likely to be remedied easily, especially in the short run.

7.1 It would be foolish then to exaggerate the importance of what broadcasting can do. Broadcasting will not create the jobs which so many young people are condemned to search for in vain. To the sort of things broadcasting *can* do, some observers see objections. For example, John Bazalgette of the Grubb Institute, thought broadcasts could easily fall into the trap of keeping young people out of trouble, thereby distracting attention from the real problem — offering 'circuses' when what is needed is 'bread'. This Report suggests ways in which broadcasting can do more than act as a palliative, emphasising however that the effectiveness of broadcasting is often critically dependent on how well its efforts are linked with the activities of other agencies. We hope that our conclusions and recommendations point towards such new strategies.

7.2 In outlining our conclusions about the possible future role of broadcasting in meeting the needs of young people, we are aware of course that 'young people' is a generalization as fictitious as it is unavoidable. Young people are not a homogeneous group — a working-class black boy in Liverpool has values, attitudes and needs that are very different from those of a middle class girl in

95

Esher. Thus, we are aware that any statements about the needs of young people must be read with caution. We have been particularly conscious of the needs of the less able young person, but most of our conclusions concern young people generally, and the various adult groups involved with them.

7.3 Young people's needs

7.3.1 We consider that many young people need help in *basic educational skills*, including literacy, numeracy and social and life skills, by which we mean principally the practical techniques of making and doing, including seeking advice, claiming entitlements, elementary budgeting, leisure needs and applying for jobs, as well as a greater understanding of oneself in relation to others.

7.3.2 Important too for many young people is help with understanding *personal relationships*, particularly those involved in the transition from the dependence of school to the independence of taking a place in the adult world; and in moving from a society relatively homogeneous in age to one in which they will have to deal with a variety of different age and interest groups.

7.3.3 Many young people, even those reasonably equipped in elementary skills, have very little understanding of *general political, social and economic matters*, or of the nature of the industrial and commercial world. Within this broad context, they need greater specific *careers education and guidance* including information about the realities of working life (physical, social, emotional) the nature of jobs, the inter-relation between job aspirations and educational requirements, the ability to develop 'job-search' skills, the opportunities for further education and training and the sources of advice and support.

7.3.4 For those who are actually unemployed, the problem is particularly acute. They frequently lack information about benefits, alternatives to employment, including voluntary work, self-help schemes, the opportunities of YOP and STEP, and so on.

7.3.5 The Government's UVP scheme seems to us to be a particularly interesting attempt to integrate the demands of further education and training, and thus more fully meets the needs of young people at work. Indeed, whilst believing that more attention should be paid to *vocational skill training* generally, we would also emphasise the application of knowledge to problem solving and the development of general manipulative skills.

7.3.6 Finally, many young people, employed and unemployed alike — and individuals often move between the groups — are relatively unprepared for adult life in terms of *exploiting the full potential of leisure*, particularly at times when they are not in work. Indeed, it seems to us that the whole notion of 'leisure' in an employment-orientated society demands much greater attention and study.

7.4 Needs of adults

7.4.1 There is a need to inform adults about the economic changes and technological innovations which will affect them as parents and as employees or employers. For example, largely thanks to television, the advent of the silicon chip has now entered the public consciousness, but awareness of its technological significance and its consequent economic impact is still slight. In fact, adult groups (and young people too) are largely unaware of the way in which knowledge is actually applied within our society.

7.4.2 Various professional workers, teachers, college lecturers, careers officers, youth and community workers, industrial coaches and trainers, declared that their services are overstretched at this time, particularly as a result of the current economic situation, and of the measures being taken by the Government and others to meet young people's needs more fully. We believe that these groups can in some degree be helped by broadcasting to make their specialist contribution to the needs of young adults.

7.5 Educational broadcasting

7.5.1 Educational broadcasters have gone further than any other single group within broadcasting to meet the needs of young people and those adults who have young people in their care. The BBC's school series *Going to Work*, for example, has made a major contribution within the field of careers education; and new programmes have been designed to help young people make the transition from school to work such as YTV's school series *Making a Living*.

7.5.2 But there is very little of use for those who have just left school, apart from a small output directed at further education colleges, such as the BBC's *Engineering Craft Studies*. There is clearly a need for educational broadcasting to be further developed not only for schools but also for young people at college or in industry-based training schemes, or currently out of work. Although some educational broadcasts intended for schools and colleges are scheduled at appropriate times, other educational broadcasts are transmitted at times when few people are available to benefit from them.

7.5.3 The BBC and the IBA and the Independent Radio and Television Companies should take more note of the important changes taking place in post-school education and training – those being developed, for example, under the YOP, STEP and UVP schemes. We believe that educational broadcasting could be given a sharper focus in relation to some of these schemes, particularly in the area of basic education material.

7.5.4 It is likely that the development of any such programmes would require substantial changes in the present television scheduling arrangements: for example, the present pattern of term-time school broadcasts might with advantage be adjusted so as to make room for this additional programming effort.

7.6 General programmes on television

7.6.1 We are forced to conclude that general programming is not providing anything like the range of output appropriate to meet the needs of young people.

7.6.2 Even so, the foundations have been laid. BBC's *Something Else* was an interesting example of an innovatory programme for young people, though it has not yet been developed beyond the pilot stage. Similarly, some existing ITV *regional* programmes for young people have explored the potential of a variety of styles and contents. These include the Thames magazine series *Pauline's People*, LWT's current affairs/features series *The London Weekend Show*, the access service for young people, *You Can Make It* (Tyne Tees), the participatory series about youth news *What's New* (Granada).

7.6.3 We believe that there is a need for *network* provision for this age group, in a variety of styles.

7.6.4 Local/regional programming for young people deserves further development in its own right. Over and over we were told that what helped young people in, say, the South West, would be of little value to the same age group in the North East. Significantly, too, the importance of liaison with local agencies, of follow up to programmes, which we have stressed elsewhere as being of key importance, is easier on a local or regional level than nationally.

7.6.5 The BBC's output is primarily networked, and thus it does not have the same potential for regional programming. Even so, we think that the National Regions should have programmes designed for young people in relation to the needs indicated in this Study. At present they do not.

7.6.6 Some of ITV's local programmes have already been mentioned but others are also worth noting, particularly those relating to unemployment. A notable example is Westward's *Just the Job*, and there are programmes with similar intentions from Ulster, HTV and other companies, with an analogue to *Just the Job* in preparation for the Scottish television area. Despite the valuable start that has been made, ITV's provision when viewed nationally, remains patchy, and could be extended.

7.6.7 Some broadcasters have attempted to justify the comparative lack of programming for young people by saying that young adults, compared with older or younger sections of the community, are light viewers. They have other things to do than watch television, we have been told. Doubtless they have – but we are left with the thought that young people may be light viewers chiefly because the present broadcast provision simply fails to engage their interest.

7.7 General programmes on radio

7.7.1 Young adults at present are listeners rather than viewers. In practice, this means they usually listen to BBC Radio 1 and to ILR. As far as national radio is concerned, Radio 1 is the only nationally transmitted radio network whose audience consists of a high proportion of young people. Although at present first and foremost a pop music network, there are a number of programme elements in its schedules which are designed to provide information and advice for young people. The extension of transmission hours into the early evening, separate from Radio 2, is being used to extend this provision. We would stress the need, mentioned elsewhere, for programmes of this kind to be supported wherever possible by non-broadcasting agencies which are able to provide extended systems of support and advice.

7.7.2 Local radio is different. It has the enormous advantage that each local station can develop its own approaches and keep close contact with its area. Its disadvantage is, sometimes, an excessive parochialism, an ignorance of the experience gained elsewhere, and of the services or support available. Taking into account the limited resources available to radio stations, a systematic exchange of information seems particularly important.

7.7.3 Although there are encouraging developments on radio in relation to young people's employment needs, the time has now come for other possible subject areas to be considered — for example, basic education and the individual's relation to industrial society — with a view to similar ingenuity being used to incorporate such matters within the popular format of the stations.

7.8 Programme style

7.8.1 Many of those to whom we have spoken during the course of the Study have commented on programme style as a key element in determining whether broadcasters are successful in reaching and influencing young people.

7.8.2 Young people themselves, and indeed adult groups too, mentioned the same programmes as illustrative of appropriate style for the young, for example, *Multi Coloured Swap Shop*, with its imaginative use of magazine style technique, or the *Kenny Everett Video Show*. They frequently mentioned the importance of humour. At another level, Capital Radio's series in *Hullabaloo* on examination set-books has illustrated that even hard-core educational material does not have to be dull and sterile.

7.8.3 'Soap operas' featuring 'ordinary' young people were seen by many informed adults as a technique for capturing interest and sympathy and providing the opportunity for 'education by stealth'. *The Archers* was frequently referred to. Others believed that folk heroes, pop stars, disc jockeys and sports personalities could help in presenting serious material which young people might otherwise dismiss without giving it a fair hearing. This may be so — we suspect that it is.

7.8.4 However, the truth is that we know very little about how young people react to any given programme style. Indeed, there is little information available about young people's attitudes in general and specifically about their reactions to the mass media. Further work needs to be done in close consultation with young people themselves. It may be that present adult hunches will turn out to be little more than adult condescension: the most trendy presentation may not be the most effective. We certainly need to find out.

7.9 Structures

7.9.1 If young people's needs are not being taken into account by broadcasting, we need to find out why. There is certainly no lack of goodwill amongst broadcasters towards the young adult. However, neither the BBC nor ITV seem at present to believe that the needs of the 14—21 age group are sufficiently distinct from those of the adult population as a whole to require any major separate broadcast provision. Indeed, in 1978 the BBC, in a report to its General Advisory Council, said so explicitly.

7.9.2 This belief is reflected in the absence of any structure within the broadcasting organisations which deal specifically with programmes for young adults. Even within educational broadcasting the 14—21 age group tends to fall across the broad remits of the Schools Broadcasting Council and Further Education Advisory Council in the case of the BBC, and between that of the Schools Committee and the Adult Education Committee in the case of the IBA. Consequently, that there is any programming at all specifically for young people results from ad hoc initiatives rather than from the broadcasting organisations' conscious desire to meet the needs of this age group.

7.9.3 We have already commented on the need to schedule programmes at times when young people (and indeed their parents) are available to view or listen. Specifically with regard to television, it is interesting to note that the IFF research pointed firmly towards a 5–7pm slot on weekdays, and to weekend scheduling, including Saturday morning.

7.9.4 Our conclusion must be that, at the moment, the structures and conventions of broadcasting itself, including scheduling policies, hinder and restrict the broadcasters' abilities to meet young people's needs.

7.10 Co-operation with agencies outside broadcasting

7.10.1 Broadcasting, as we have said, is far from being the only, or indeed, the principal agency concerned with young people. During the course of this Study we have been struck by the large number of such agencies, many with the same aims.

7.10.2 Although broadcasting, as one element, can do something for young people on its own, it can do much more when it works in conjunction with others who care to follow up and provide support beyond the programme itself. Strategies of linkage might, for example, involve partnership with a range of outside agencies (correspondence colleges, volunteer agencies, further and higher education, and the producers of popular print material — newspapers, comics and magazines) in order to make provision for direct help and advice.

7.10.3 Over the last year or two there have been several initiatives which, though not specifically for young people and in the main restricted to educational programmes, have shown that broadcasters can find such 'partners' willing to accept the work and/or financial burden of following up or giving other support to a broadcast. The MSC, for example, has frequently provided invaluable support to programmes by funding print-materials or the manning of telephones and so on. Consequently, relatively modest initiatives in television terms, such as Westward's *Just the Job* have achieved a social, economic and political dimension far beyond the starting point of the programmes alone.

7.10.4 We believe that if the MSC is to continue its supportive role, and if non-governmental agencies such as the National Extension College, the Scottish Community Education Centre, or the National Youth Bureau are to be encouraged to continue working with broadcasters in the future, it will be necessary to structure the idea of partnership beyond the present ad hoc arrangements.

7.10.5 We fear that the weaknesses implicit in present arrangements cannot be eradicated simply by internal reorganisation or external liaison. There is no consistent or systematic method of bringing educators, employers, youth workers and young people themselves together with the broadcasters for task-orientated activities − nothing, in short, that acts as a sort of 'junction-box'. Nor is there any service capable of providing the co-ordination or back-up for joint schemes which require support of print material or the organisation of counselling and information services.

7.10.6 We conclude, therefore, that there will soon be a need for a central organisation to bring together on a working basis those who are concerned to help young people in association with the media. It should be a youth-orientated venture with interest in media rather than the reverse. The development of such an organisation is not primarily a matter for the broadcasters, but for those agencies concerned with helping young people.

8 Recommendations

8.0 Before turning to specific recommendations, we would like to make three **general recommendations**. First, during the course of the Study we have found little hard information about young people in relation to the media. We therefore **recommend** that research should be promoted to clarify patterns of use and response among young people in relation to popular media. In the case of radio and television, such research might usefully be extended to investigate the effectiveness of various alternative styles of programming.

8.1 Second, the importance of stable relationships and of adequate provision for the emotional and leisure needs of young adults were emphasised to us again and again as essential components of any provision to help young adults acquire additional skills and move easily from school to work. More information is needed in this field however, suggesting the need for a second stage to this Study. We **recommend**, therefore, that the Gulbenkian Foundation extends its current concern for educational disadvantage in the 14–25 age group by consulting with appropriate agencies to initiate further enquiry into the social situation of young adults today, including their emotional and leisure needs, and to concert action.

8.2 Third, we believe that the 14–21 age group does have needs distinct from the totality of the adult population and that broadcasters should accept responsibility to respond to these needs.

8.3 Our **specific recommendations** fall into two parts:

> those requiring action by broadcasters alone, and
> those requiring additional action by other agencies or by broadcasters in partnership with other agencies.

8.4 Recommendations requiring action principally by broadcasters

8.4.1 *Television*

8.4.1.1 We **recommend** that the BBC, the IBA and the ITV Companies should examine and if necessary, alter their present organisational structures to ensure that arrangements exist which encourage a coherent response to the needs of the 14–21 age group.

8.4.1.2 We **recommend** that current broadcast provision for young adults should be developed in two ways.

i   There should be more 'general output' *popular* and informative programmes for young adults. We suggest that such programmes should be scheduled at times when young people (and their parents) are available to view at home – for instance, weekend mornings especially Saturdays, or between 5 and 7 pm during the week.

ii   Extra broadcast provision should be made for the *educational* needs of young adults. New programming effort is required, particularly in the area of basic education, including literacy, numeracy and social and life skills. Programmes would be additionally effective if planned for potential use in the Youth Opportunities Programme, Special Temporary Employment Programme and Unified Vocational Preparation courses and linked to in-service material for appropriate professional groups.

Present scheduling would need to be reconsidered to accommodate these needs.

8.4.1.3 In local/regional programming, both educational and general, we **recommend** that ITV should take greater advantage of its federal strength to develop a pattern of local coverage in those areas of programming (*eg* unemployment) where local need is critical.

8.4.1.4 Further we **recommend** that current developments within BBC Scotland, Wales and Northern Ireland and any projected developments in the English regions, should include a reassessment of priorities to allow for programmes designed specifically for young people.

8.4.1.5 In particular, we **recommend** that these programmes, whether 'educational' or 'general', networked or local, should, where possible and when appropriate, be developed in co-operation with external voluntary and statutory agencies, to provide programme follow-up and support activities.

8.4.2 *Radio*

8.4.2.1 We note the appeal of radio to young people, particularly Radio 1 and ILR. We **recommend** that Radio 1's present development to provide more programmes giving information and advice, should be backed up by the creation of a substantial support service.

8.4.2.2 In local radio, we **recommend** that the BBC on the one hand and the IBA and ILR Companies on the other, should investigate separately some mechanism for channelling detailed background information about employment and unemployment, training schemes, the Youth Opportunities Programme and so on, from which might be provided a common service for each of their systems.

8.4.2.3 We **recommend** that local radio stations should develop further close contacts with youth agencies of all kinds as a useful preliminary to future collaboration over a wider range of topics than at present.

8.4.3 *General*

8.4.3.1 We **recommend** that the IBA, the Companies and the BBC should consider how, separately or jointly, they might

    i   establish more regular connections with external agencies with a view to increasing in number and effectiveness the programmes which link broadcasts with other parallel efforts (see 8.5 below);

ii improve arrangements for referring viewers/listeners to the agencies which have been involved already.

8.5 Recommendations requiring action either by other agencies or by broadcasting in conjunction with other agencies

8.5.1 We **recommend** that the substantial and critically important contribution made by the MSC to support broadcasts designed to help young people should be continued and extended.

8.5.2 We endorse the recommendation in Paragraph 168 of the House of Commons Report on *The Attainment of the School Leaver*. Consequently, we **recommend** that the DES should encourage those agencies (including broadcasters) concerned with young people to develop "the promotion and evaluation of moderately sized schemes of non-traditional post-compulsory education".

8.5.3 We **recommend** that voluntary and statutory organisations in conjunction with the broadcasters, should explore how programme strands (both 'educational' and 'general') can be followed up more regularly and effectively by supporting print and other activities — bearing in mind the needs of young people and the adults who have them in their care.

8.5.4 We **recommend** that the funding of these collaborative support activities should be met by whichever source is appropriate, including the public purse.

8.5.5 Keeping in mind cheapness and availability, we **recommend** that the appropriate agencies should investigate the possibilities of an increased use of audio and video cassettes in schools, colleges, and industrial and commercial training schemes — and when feasible, within the home.

8.5.6 Although all our recommendations seem to build on existing practice, we believe that such practice is in many ways ad hoc. Therefore, we **recommend** that the MSC and the broadcasting organisations together with other appropriate agencies, should take a primary role in the formation of a Young Adult Unit. This Unit might fulfil, initially, urgent short term tasks like gathering and disseminating information which is not at present available, (*eg* section 8.0) or providing a co-ordinating/evaluative role in one of several relevant initiatives currently under discussion. These initiatives seem to us to provide the basis for a new collaborative strategy, the development of which is essential if the needs of young people are to be met in each of the areas we have defined. To sum up, therefore, the principal role of a Young Adult Unit would be to help stimulate collaboration and co-ordinate action between the media and young adults; provide channels of communication between the two and the general public; and especially, help formulate and present the young adults' needs to all concerned.

Part IV

Appendices

Appendix I Structure of broadcasting

The BBC

The bulk of the BBC's television and radio national output is produced in London. However in addition to this network output, Scotland, Wales and Northern Ireland have significant and growing television and radio outputs of their own which are separately funded and transmitted. The consequence of this growth is fairly certain to be a much greater ability on the part of the Controllers of each 'National Region' to reflect the individual character of their areas. There are in addition, within England, eight regional broadcasting centres, which initiate their own television and radio output. Although covering areas and populations as big as, or bigger than, the National Regions, these English centres are much more limited in terms of staff and resources and are principally concerned with news and current affairs programmes.

There are also twenty BBC Local Radio stations — all in England. Responsibility for the programme policy of each station rests with the Station Manager and since each local radio station is separately funded, this results in a major degree of independence from the London based radio output.

Independent Broadcasting

The Independent Broadcasting Authority provides all the Independent Television and Independent Local Radio services in the UK and covers the work of sixteen television companies (including ITN) and nineteen local radio stations. The policy of the IBA with regard to television is that its service should adequately reflect the tastes and outlook of the country as a whole and not just the metropolis. The regional dimension is thus an important one and consequently the country is divided into fourteen ITV areas, each served by its own company. Each company (there are two in London) is thus strongly identified with a region and is required by the IBA to reflect this in its programme service.

Of these companies, five, the so-called major companies, produce a core of networked television programmes in addition to their local programmes. The primary task of the remaining ten is to produce programmes for specific local appeal and then to participate in the activities of the ITV system as a whole and, in varying degrees, make their contribution to the network. The Independent Television system is, therefore, a complex one, being both plural and federal.

The nineteen Independent Local Radio stations which exist throughout the UK are, like their television counterparts, separate companies, responsible to the IBA.

Who decides what goes on air?

The BBC

Both television and national radio are separately financed and organised as Directorates. Policy is co-ordinated at a Board of Management level. Production staff are appointed to a given department such as drama, current affairs, sport, further education, religious programmes and work within the limits of that department's remit. These departments usually have no established right to air time on the networks and it is frequently necessary for the heads of the departments to win the advance approval of the channel or network controller (for example, the Controller of BBC 1 or the Controller of Radio 4) in order to secure the transmission of any programme or series. Thus national programmes produced in London emerge on the air in the context of departmental remits and in forms acceptable to the channel or network controller.

Independent Broadcasting

The key group within the Independent Television system is the Programmes Controllers Group consisting of members of the five 'major' companies — (Thames, LWT, ATV, Granada, Yorkshire) together with the IBA's Director of Television and The Director of the Network Programmes Secretariat. Together they draw up a basic schedule which is then offered to the companies for them to adjust in accordance to the needs and interests of their own local audience. All such schedules must be agreed between the IBA and the companies. Thus the programmes that eventually go on air arise from a delicate balance of local initiative, network pressures and IBA approval.

Within the Independent Local Radio system each station is responsible for its own schedules subject to the approval of the IBA.

Who, in broadcasting, is specifically concerned with young people?

The *BBC* has

i a children's television department whose target audience has an upper age limit of twelve. There is no radio equivalent and no 'youth' department for the over twelves in either television or radio;

ii school television and radio departments are concerned with all school age groups. Further education radio and television departments, whilst existing to provide educational series for adults of all ages make a regular provision for young people studying in colleges of further education, with special emphasis on the vocational implications of their courses;

iii other departments or units, for example Community Programmes, may produce series for young people as and when they choose – subject to the approval of the channel or network controller;

iv all BBC local radio stations have an education producer who is responsible for, among other things, producing series for schools, etc.

Each *Independent Television and Radio* station has its own internal structure and there is a tendency for each company to concentrate on different areas of programming. Nevertheless, to generalise, Independent Television, like the BBC, has

i children's departments, whose target audience usually has an upper age limit of about fourteen;

ii education departments for both schools and post-school provision;

iii units within certain departments that are specifically concerned with programmes for young people, for example, *The London Weekend Show* team within the LWT features department.

There are no specific youth departments or education departments within the Independent Local Radio stations, although some ILR stations have especially designated education staff.

Advisory structures

It is worth noting that both the BBC and the IBA, in addition to their general advisory structures, have specialist educational advisory procedures centred on the Schools Broadcasting Council and the Further Education Advisory Council in the case of the BBC, and the Educational Advisory Council, a Schools Committee and an Adult Education Committee in the case of the IBA.

Further information about this or any other aspect of the operation of the broadcasting organisations can be obtained from the BBC and IBA handbooks.

Appendix II Summary of research by Industrial Facts and Forecasting Ltd

Although we have referred to this research elsewhere, readers may be interested not only to learn how this was carried out but also to have some additional evidence from the materials gathered.

The research was carried out in Enfield (London), Swansea, Sheffield, Leeds and the Newcastle area. Employers were selected to represent types of employment open to sixteen year old school leavers in the area. The young people interviewed had all left school in the past two years at sixteen and a substantial proportion were unemployed. The research method used was to hold separate group discussions not only with personnel managers and people in similar positions, but also with young people themselves. Finally, a number of individual in-depth interviews were carried out.

Young people

When young people were asked about their experiences since leaving school including looking for jobs, virtually all those interviewed said they had not enjoyed their last year at school and many had not attended regularly. The obligation to turn up to work every day and face the restrictions involved in working life was difficult for young people to adjust to at first. The following comment was typical.

> "No, I was pretty regular in school like, but if I wanted a day off like, and difficulty getting out of bed like — it wouldn't worry you. You just wouldn't bother to go in. They wouldn't sack you from school like — but with work like, you've got to go in every day like."

Many felt they were ill-prepared for the world of work and wished that the teachers had imposed stricter discipline and offered more insight into what to expect. Many claimed never to have seen a careers officer at school — although this claim may reveal more about their attitudes than the service they did or did not experience. Many young people said they preferred to find jobs by themselves or with the help of family and friends as this gave them a sense of independence. Those who had seen career officers had a mixed reaction to the advice they had received both before and after leaving school. Some found the careers service helpful, others complained about being pressurised into jobs they didn't want. They commented too on a lack of guidance if they were not sure what job they wanted.

114

Virtually all the young people interviewed by IFF wanted to work, both for the sake of independence and self-respect, and because they had a dread of the depressing aspects of unemployment, of parental disapproval, boredom and demoralisation.

> "Being on the dole depressed you a lot — or depressed me anyway — I felt awful. I got to a stage you know where everything and everybody was getting on my nerves, even my dog."

They were asked what advice they would give school leavers. Most said, "Stay at school and get your qualifications". Many advised against settling for just any job and thought it was better to stay on at school or keep trying until the right job was decided on and found. Teachers might do well to invite back into school some of their more reluctant pupils who are now on the labour market.

Employers

The employers interviewed remarked, as did the young people, on the difficulties experienced in adjusting to working life. Absenteeism was mentioned and they also felt that the dangers of the work place and the consequent need for discipline were not appreciated sufficiently by young people.

> "I have seen in one instance a lad driving a fork lift truck — it was lunchtime — and playing St George and the dragon with it chasing the other drivers with the forks up. That is the sort of thing that happens; one can expect it with the younger generation, but when one criticises them and tries to take them through it — it is not good saying 'Stop that'. You have to take them back and say that the thing is like a tank, it runs over you and just leaves you flat — when you walk away from them, the comment virtually is 'Do you think we are back at school again?' "

Despite this, most employers claimed to welcome much closer contact with schools and thought work experience schemes a good idea.

Attitudes to broadcasting

Most of the young people, as one might expect, preferred listening to pop music on the radio — almost exclusively they listened to BBC Radio 1 and ILR stations which they identified as being geared to young people's interests. Independent radio, in particular, was favoured both for its youth programmes and for its local content. They did not care for 'talking' programmes, although phone-ins and job information were tolerated.

By the standards of their parents, or younger brothers and sisters, they tended to be light viewers — although it is important to bear in mind that 'light' is a relative term — and their viewing was usually restricted to tea-time (between 5 and 7 pm) and sometimes late at night. Weekends were also mentioned. The unemployed also watched television in the afternoon.

Favourite programmes were light comedy, films and 'action' series. News and current affairs programmes were almost universally disliked. However, local magazine programmes, including local news programmes, were popular. There were some differences in programme tastes between the girls and boys. Most girls interviewed were 'addicts' of either *Crossroads* or *Coronation Street*, neither of which interested the boys. On the other hand, the girls were uninterested in football, which the boys enjoyed watching. These findings broadly support the evidence put forward in Chapter 3 of this Study.

Both employers and young people were asked what part they thought broadcasting could play in meeting specific needs. Young people felt that broadcasting could give them more realistic information about the range of jobs available and what each job involved.

> "Television, you know pictures . . . watching the television you learn more, more than you learn off the teacher, you know, watching it."

> "Well it gives the practical side of it can't it, where as with a teacher it is just . . . they just chat on."

It was felt that present programmes and careers booklets did not give a vivid enough picture of both the good and bad aspects of a job. Young people also thought that TV programmes could give guidance on how to set about getting a job; handling the interview and so on. Radio would be more appropriate in giving local job information, although the respondents felt that the descriptions of jobs should be much more detailed than that in current 'job spots'.

They also thought broadcasting could help with other problems such as money management and relationships with parents. They liked the idea of showing young people discussing relationships with parents.

> "Yes, because then you see it, they are more or less you, they talk about what you really feel, because they are going through the same thing."

And again, specifically in the context of parental attitudes to unemployment,

> "I think it would give them a chance to see what problems we are going through. I think there are so many parents who just think 'she is a layabout — she doesn't want to do it, she is just turning work down.' "

Certainly the style of programme presentation was held to be very important. Most young people thought pop music should be used as a 'hook'. There was some disagreement about the right age for presenters, although all agreed that it should be someone who 'seemed young', and someone they could identify with — Noel Edmonds was mentioned as a suitable presenter, for example. A token young adult was no good at all . . . When asked whether it was felt that young people themselves should be involved in programmes, one young person replied,

"If they done them natural like, but in both these programmes with young people they have got some stuck-up little poof in the chair with a bit of paper in front of him all lah-di-dah. Who would watch that? Why can't they have someone else for a change? Someone scruffy or something."

Interestingly, the employers' views about the role broadcasting could play in meeting specific needs were broadly in agreement with those comments from the young people. They agreed that television could give young people a clearer idea of what was involved in various jobs, provided they did not glamourise them. IFF reports on the comments made by our employers about a training film made by the International Wool Secretariat.

"The informant was very indignant that the film began and ended with peaceful rural scenes of sheep grazing and lambs frolicking, which he felt was very misleading, it glamourised what were noisy and dirty jobs, rather than presenting them as they are."

The employers also agreed that television could show young people how to go about getting a job. There was some disagreement, however, about the best setting for showing such programmes. Some felt it was the school's responsibility and that young people would not watch such programmes in their own time. Others felt that it was counter-productive to let 'careers' programmes become identified with school and suggested early evening viewing at home. There was also some discussion on whether broadcasting might be used as an element within induction and initial training schemes in industry. The employers thought that a personal approach would usually be more effective and as there was too much variation between individual firms to make such induction programmes practicable. They believed however that programmes could be developed which would provide valuable background information on the nature of our industrial society. Similarly they thought that broadcasting could draw attention to the need for competence in basic skills.

From the employers' point of view the main job which broadcasting could do would be to counteract the unreal image of industrial jobs which they considered was put forward by teachers who lacked sympathy, experience or understanding of life on the shop floor. It would also introduce young people to the realities before they left school so that they would not be so easily disillusioned on starting work.

"The role of broadcasting is to try and give them some idea of what work is all about. It's a hell of a jump going from school to work. All young people are petrified of making the wrong decision in taking a job."

During the course of the IFF discussions and interviews young people were given the opportunity to see and listen to various types of youth programmes in order to stimulate discussion about what they liked or didn't like in the existing broadcast provision. Thus extracts were chosen at random from various series but it is worth noting that a clip from BBC2's *Something Else* was preferred by informants as it was presented by young people, covered topics relevant to their needs and had an attractive style of presentation including music and graphics.

Appendix III Westward TV's *Just the Job*

The *Just the Job* project has been mentioned a number of times in this Report as an example of the sort of broadcast based initiative we think is particularly useful to young people. *Just the Job* is now in its second year in the South West of England. It aims to reach out to the isolated young unemployed, (in a predominantly rural area) who are out of touch with statutory agencies, and to interest them in doing something to help themselves. The 1977 project aroused interest through 7 TV programmes which were transmitted in the early evening (5.15 pm) in November/December. Each programme encouraged the viewer to phone a Freefone number in order to obtain a free Jobhunter Kit and to join a group of young unemployed people led by an adult volunteer. The kits and groups were designed to help young people think through their problems and to reach a decision on what action they were going to take. On reaching a decision the young person made contact with the appropriate statutory agencies, but was able to do so with the social support of the group behind him/her. Thus the service was not designed to supplement statutory agencies but to assist young people to use them more effectively.

At the time of the 1977 transmission there were about 8–10,000 young (16–17 year olds) unemployed in the South West. The programmes resulted in 2572 referrals of which 1110 were in the target group and of these 77% (857) agreed to join groups. Thus around 10% of the target group entered counselling groups. Of those young people who joined groups, 49% moved on to some opportunity and the general benefits of all group members were identified as

- improved morale and confidence
- improved interview and job search skills
- more regular and constructive use of agencies
- better understanding of their situations
- a sharing of their problems and anxieties
  better understanding of all the local resources and employment opportunities
- improved understanding of the government's 'special measures'

The 1978 project incorporates extensive modifications to the television programmes and to the way the programmes link to the project and it is expected that these will lead to a much higher rate of group participation.

119

The TV series is to consist of six programmes which are to be broadcast at 5.20 pm on Thursdays and repeated on the following Saturdays at noon. On the basis of feed-back from the pilot project, the programmes are to be shortened from 30 minutes to 20 minutes in length and the format has been re-modelled to include more light-hearted visual material and fewer interviews. Some topics which were felt to be too ambitious for the capacity of the viewers, such as information on how to set up your own business, have been dropped. The general line which the programmes take is one of "it's not your fault you're unemployed − don't give up hope, keep plugging away".

The Programmes

The themes of each of the six programmes are broadly as follows:

Programme 1: Why bother to work?
While being unemployed may seem to have its advantages when the sun is shining, when other people are stuck in offices and factories, it also has its less attractive aspects and these are spelt out in the programme.

Programme 2: Attitude of mind
This programme is addressed to those who have tried in vain to get a job and have given up in despair. It attempts to encourage a more positive attitude and includes a number of practical suggestions for avenues which might be tried.

Programme 3: Using the system
This programme concentrates on information about the opportunities which are available: YOP, WEP Training Workshops, community work, etc.

Programme 4: Get a training
This programme spells out the advantages in the job market of having undergone some form of training and gives information about courses available at technical colleges, etc.

Programme 5: That interview
This programme gives advice on self-assessment, 'selling' yourself to an employer, how to handle an interview and so on.

Programme 6: Use your spare time
The theme of this programme is that even if all else fails you may as well put your spare time to some positive use. It also points out that developing proficiency in a hobby may well impress an employer, and may also in some cases be a practical preparation for a job.

As few people are likely to watch the whole series, all the programmes contain material about YOP and the work experience programme. Other material is also recapitulated.

The Jobhunter Kits

Jobhunter 1: Why unemployment?
Cartoon style exploration of structural changes taking place in employment.

Jobhunter 2: Getting organised
Part 1:   The agencies. A guide to the statutory agencies available to help young people.
Part 2:   Jobsearch skills.

Jobhunter 3: Youth opportunities programme
A cartoon style explanation of YOP.

Jobhunter 4: Time on your hands?
Guide to further education and training provision.

Jobhunter 5: Lively unemployment
Voluntary work and earning within the £2 limit.

Jobhunter 6: Doing your own thing
Setting up your own opportunity.

Other components

It is worth noting that although, as in the 1977 pilot scheme, the project consists of a television series backed up by printed Jobhunter Kits and a network of 100 voluntary counsellors, this second stage has two additional elements.

1.   In the Plymouth area, Plymouth Sound (the local ILR station) will broadcast in part of its Tuesday evening pop show, over a ten week period, information about local opportunities including work experience, YOP, counselling and such job opportunities as are available;

2.   In the Cornwall area, a local newspaper is to produce a pull-out centrefold of similar information for young people.

The broadcast elements of the 1978 project will, once again, be produced and paid for by all the companies concerned. The other elements are to be funded, as was the case in the 1977 project, by the MSC.

Appendix IV Individuals and organisations consulted by the Study Officers

We wish to extend our warmest thanks to all the people who have helped us in the course of the Study, not only those whose names appear below but also many members of the broadcasting organisations and the MSC, who are too numerous to mention individually.

Geoffrey Abraham	Essex County Inspectorate
Kenneth Adams	St Georges Conference Centre, Windsor
Chris Allenson	Community Projects Foundation
David Ashton	Leicester University
Richard Ayres	British Association for Commercial and Industrial Education
Sophie Balhatchet	Association of Independent Producers
Tim Barnes	Community Service Volunteers
Harry Barrington	Lever Brothers
Miss N Bartman	Department of Education and Science
F Barwise	Dean High School, Bolton
Mike Bayes	South Thames College
John Bazalgette	Grubb Institute of Behavioural Studies
Michael Bennett	Education Department, Coventry
Len Bill	City and Guilds of London Institute
William Blease	Formerly of Northern Ireland TUC
David Blezzard	Nelson and Colne College
Bill Boaden	National Association of Teachers in Further and Higher Education
Richard Bourne	Evening Standard
Avtar Brah	National Association for Asian Youth
Bernard Branch	Careers Office, Education Department, Sheffield
Chris Brooks	Youthaid
Clive Brooks	Radyr Comprehensive, Radyr
Ray Burton	Education Department, Isle of Wight
Eileen Byrne	Equal Opportunities Commission
Terry Carlan	Northern Ireland TUC
Helen Carter	Schools Council
W G Carter	Education Department, Sheffield
Bob Coulter	IBA Fellow
Jack Chambers	National Union of Teachers

Ruby Chambers	Rubber and Plastics Processing ITB
Louis Chase	Full Employ
Neville Cheetham	National Youth Bureau
Mike Clark	The New University of Ulster
Peter Clyne	I L E A
David Coffey	Vocational Guidance Dept, Belfast Polytechnic
Yvonne Collemore	MUS CRE Caribbean Literacy Project, Westminster
G Collins	Deane Grammar School, Bolton
Terry Collins	Careers Officer, Wiltshire County Council
K H J Cook	Careers Officer, Newport, Isle of Wight
Charles Cooper	Contemporary Films Ltd
E Cordell	Department of Education and Science
Ann Coulson	Bromsgrove College
Paul Curno	Gulbenkian Foundation
Joe Curran	Department of Manpower Services Northern Ireland
Ann Daniel	*Daily Telegraph* Careers Information Service
Ed Darcy	Community Education, Paisley
Guy Dauncey	Freelance writer
J H Davies	Welsh Joint Education Centre
H W B Davies	Department of Education and Science
J D Dawson	Department of Education and Science
Barry Deller	*Just the Job* team, Dartington
Paddy Doherty	Derry Youth and Community Workshop, Northern Ireland
John Donaghy	Youthways, Northern Ireland
R N Drewery	George Tomlinson County Secondary School, Bolton
Margaret Dunn	Manchester Polytechnic
Maurice Edmundson	Department of Education and Science
R Fell	Rivington and Blackrod High School, Bolton
Peter Fiddick	*The Guardian*
Dorothy Flemming	Sheffield City Polytechnic
Fred Flower	Kingsway Princeton College, I L E A
John Garrett	H M I, Cardiff
Alan Gibson	H M I
Marion Giordan	Consultant Consumer Education
Tom Griffiths	Devon Centre, Dartington
Brian Groombridge	Extra Mural Department, London University
Pat Haikin	South Thames College
Marjorie Haddill	Confederation of British Industry, Wales
John Harding	Devon Probation and Aftercare Service
Jeremy Harrison	Community Projects Foundation
A Henderson	Castle Hill (Girls) High School, Bolton
Mike Hodgkinson	Volunteer Centre Media Project
Pat Holland	*Society Today*
Brenda Howe	Leeds Education Department
David Howie	National Youth Bureau

Mathew Jack	HMI, Scotland
Ravi Jain	National Association for Asian Youth
Simon Jenkin	Schools Department, Essex
Rachel Jenkins	Bedfordshire Education Committee (seconded to Basic Education Committee for ACACE)
H C H Jones	Department of Education and Science
Morris Kaufmann	Rubber and Plastics Processing ITB
Bob Kedney	Wirral Metropolitan Authority
Margaret Korving	Writer and broadcaster on careers
Jane King	Centre for Information and Advice on Educational Disadvantage, Manchester
Alan Lambourne	Education Department, Sheffield
Jack Lavelle	Priory School, Lundwood, Barnsley
Tony Lavin	Bolton Teachers' Centre
Marcus Liddle	Scottish Community Education Centre
David Logan	Youthaid
Gerry Loughran	Department of Manpower Services, Northern Ireland
Martin Lightfoot	School Council Industry Project
David Mallen	Education Department, Coventry
Peter Mandelson	British Youth Council
S E McClelland	HMCI, Scotland
Christine McKay	Community Education, Paisley
Joyce McKay	School of Further Education, Jordanhill, Glasgow
Jim McKinney	Scottish Community Education Centre
Danny McNeill	Department of Manpower Services, Northern Ireland
John Meed	National Extension College
Ralph Mellon	School of Further Education, Jordanhill, Glasgow
Allen Mercer	Scottish Community Education Centre
Eric Midwinter	National Consumer Council
Tony Miles	Coventry Waterways Project
Jeremy Mitchell	National Consumer Council
Leslie Morphy	National Union of Students
John Morrison	Careers Office, Fife
Stephen Murgatroyd	Educational Resources Information Centre, Cardiff
Gerald Normie	Open University
Errol Nott	*The Daily Telegraph*
Gordon Oakes	Minister of State, Department of Education and Science
Jos Owen	Education Department, Devon
Anna Patterson	Educational Resources Information Centre, Cardiff
Mike Phillips	Journalist and broadcaster
James Platt	Central Bureau for Educational Visits and Exchange

124

Russell Possitt	Lewisham Councillor
Marion Prescott	City and East London College
Davina Prince	National Extension College
Jim Radford	Manchester Council of Voluntary Services, Manchester
Jane Reed	*Woman's Own*
Barry Reeves	Just the Job team, Dartington
Martin Roebuck	HMI Scotland
Alan Rogers	Workers Education Association
Rodney Rose	Careers and Occupational Information Centre
C W Rowland	Department of Education and Science
Mike Salmon	Chelmer Institute
Philip Samuel	HMI
Gerald Sanctuary	Law Society
A P Sandy	Education Department, Coventry
Mike Scally	Counselling and Careers Development Unit, University of Leeds
Chris Shellard	Tottenham Polytechnic
Liz Shields	North East London Polytechnic
Brian Simpson	Bellingham Middle School, Northumberland
Joe Simpson	Community Service Volunteers
Sue Slipman	National Union of Students
Sir Alec Smith	Manchester Polytechnic
Reg Smith	City and East London College
Ralph C Smith	Continuing Education, Open University
J Stark	School of Further Education, Jordanhill, Glasgow
Doreen Stephens	Chairman, Steering Committee, Towards an Association for Broadcasters, Voluntary Organisations and Statutory Organisations involved in Social Action
John Stone	Plymouth Polytechnic
Graham Swain	National Youth Bureau
Keith Taylor	Community Project Foundation
Godfrey Thomas	Education Department, South Glamorgan
Ray Thorogood	Further Education and Curriculum Review and Development Unit
George Tolley	Sheffield Polytechnic
G W Turner	Isle of Wight Industrial Group Training Scheme, Newport
Eileen Ware	Volunteer Centre Media Project
Peter Warr	University of Sheffield
Tony Watts	National Institute of Careers and Education Guidance Counselling
Alan Wells	Adult Literacy Resource Agency
Douglas Weir	Education Department, Glasgow University
S Whalley	Little Lever County Secondary School, Bolton
Pat White	Careers Office, ILEA
Fred Williams	Younghelp, Northern Ireland
Ray Williams	Caludon Castle Comprehensive School,

Appendix IV

Peter Williamson	Community Education Officer, Lothian Region
Graham Wilson	H M I, Scottish Education Department
Mrs V Wilson	Schools Council, Cardiff
Anthell Wong	MUS Outreach Project, Paddington College

Glossary

ALRA – Adult Literacy Resource Agency
See Adult Literacy Unit

ALSSF – Adult Literacy Support Services Fund
The Adult Literacy Support Services Fund, a charitable organisation, provides a nation-wide confidential referral service for adults in support of all media activities, aimed at improving reading and writing skills, the ability to comprehend and use numbers and to communicate in English. The Fund promotes tutor training activities, publishes resource material and fosters research into aspects of book design and typography for the new reader.

ALU – Adult Literacy Unit
Set up in April 1978 to continue the work of the Adult Literacy Resource Agency in allocating Government finance to schemes for Adult Literacy.

ATTI
See National Association of Teachers in Further and Higher Education

BBC – British Broadcasting Corporation
See Appendix I

BBC Local Radio Stations
See list at end of Glossary

BYC – British Youth Council
The British Youth Council is the national co-ordinating body for all national voluntary youth organisations including the traditional voluntary bodies, national student organisations, and the youth wings of the political parties. The Council is regarded as the representative voice in international affairs of organised British Youth and is the representative in Britain of the Council of European National Youth Committees (CENYC).

Calouste Gulbenkian Foundation
Calouste Sarkis Gulbenkian was an Armenian born in Turkey in 1869. He became a British citizen, conducting much of his work from London, then settled finally in Portugal. There, a year after his death in 1955, was established the Foundation which bears his name, with purposes which are

127

'charitable, artistic, educational and scientific'. The United Kingdom and Commonwealth Branch is the only branch maintained by the Foundation outside Portugal.

Careers Service
Advisory service offered by Local Authorities since 1973. Primarily responsible for vocational guidance and first job placement to all who are in full-time education or part-time vocational education (ie all institutions except universities). Also responsible for providing continuing guidance and placing in further education, training and employment to all under 65 in theory — but in practice to young people up to about the mid-20's.

CBI — Confederation of British Industry
The Confederation was formed in 1965 by the amalgamation of the Federation of British Industries, the British Employers' Confederation and the National Association of British Manufacturers. It is the central employers' organisation which the Government consults in all matters affecting industry and commerce. The Confederation publishes a quarterly *Education and Training Bulletin*.

CEC — Scottish Community Education Centre
The Scottish Community Education Centre was established in July 1977 by the merger of the former 'Board for Information on Youth and Community Service' and 'Enterprise Youth'. The Centre's purpose is to support the development of community education in Scotland, particularly through the provision of information, advisory and training services. CEC's governing body is responsible to the Secretary of State for Scotland and is composed of nominees of Central and Local Government, voluntary organisations and related agencies. The Centre is an educational charity, limited by guarantee.

CGLI — City and Guilds of London Institute
City and Guilds is an independent body incorporated by Royal Charter. The Institute offers examinations and awards certificates on published regulations and syllabuses in a wide range of technical subjects at various levels, eg operative, craft and technician. Advisory committees, representing industry and education, develop these syllabuses, which also form the basis of courses of further education in technical colleges, colleges of art and other establishments of further education in the UK and Eire and overseas.

COI — Central Office of Information
A Government organisation staffed by multi-media information specialists with the dual role of providing information and publicity services in the UK on behalf of Government departments and other publicly financed bodies; and producing and disseminating official information overseas on behalf of the foreign and Commonwealth offices, particularly in support of exports. At home it conducts Government, press, TV, radio and poster advertising, produces booklets, leaflets, films, radio and TV material (including radio and TV 'fillers' on public service themes), exhibits photographs, etc and distributes Whitehall departmental press notices.

128

CPF – Community Projects Foundation
The Community Projects Foundation was established at the end of 1967 as the Young Volunteer Force Foundation and is a national community work and youth work agency, combining local service through small agencies with national initiatives via the central unit in London. The organisation's main objective is to promote a more equitable society through an educative process, using professional local and national project staff to stimulate community action and to enable people to provide services and influence policies themselves.

FECRDU – Further Education Curriculum Review and Development Unit
The Further Education Curriculum Review and Development Unit is an advisory, intelligence and development body for further education. It was established in 1977 by the Secretary of State for Education and Science to make possible a more co-ordinated and cohesive approach to curriculum development in FE by 1. reviewing the range of existing curricula and identifying overlap, duplication and deficiencies 2. determining priorities for action to improve the total provision and suggesting ways in which improvement can be effected 3. carrying out specific studies, helping with curricular experiments and contributing to the evaluation of objectives and 4. disseminating information about the process of curriculum development in FE.

The Grubb Institute
The Grubb Institute was set up in 1969 to carry out applied social research into the functioning of groups, organisations and communities. It is an independent company, registered as an educational charity, offering its services to individuals and organisations through advisory work, research projects and a conference programme in group relations.

IBA – Independent Broadcasting Authority
See Appendix I

IFF – Industrial Facts and Forecasting Limited
Market research organisation specialising in survey research in industrial and manpower fields (now IFF Research Ltd.)

ILR – Independent Local Radio
See list at end of Glossary

Independent Television Companies
See list at end of Glossary

Local Radio Stations
See list at end of Glossary

MSC – Manpower Services Commission
MSC was set up on 1 January 1974 under the Employment and Training Act 1973 to run the public employment and training services. The Commission, which is separate from Government but accountable to the Secretary of

State for Employment, has ten members. The Commission's chief executive functions are to help people train for and obtain jobs which satisfy their aspirations and abilities, and to help employers find suitable workers. The Commission has three main operational Divisions. 1. Employment Service (formerly ESA) 2. Training Services (formerly TSA) and 3. Special Programmes (Youth Opportunities Programme (YOP), Special Temporary Employment Programme (STEP)). Over and above these executive functions the Commission advises the Government on manpower policy issues and, with the agreement of the Government, has set itself the long term aim of developing a comprehensive manpower policy with a dual function 1. to enable the country's manpower resources to be developed and contribute fully to economic well-being and 2. to ensure that there is available to each worker the opportunities and services he or she needs in order to lead a satisfying working life. The Commission's activities are financed from public funds but fees are charged for certain services.

NATFHE – National Association of Teachers in Further and Higher Education (formerly ATTI) Professional trade union for teachers in Further and Higher Education to represent their career, educational and professional needs.

NCSS – National Council of Social Service
The Council develops co-operation among voluntary social agencies and between them and statutory authorities; assists in the training of voluntary workers and provides training courses in community work for its own staff and those of affiliated organisations.

NEC – National Extension College
Registered as a non-profit-making educational charity, the NEC conducts correspondence courses covering many O and A level subjects, preparatory courses for the Open University, and others. There is a University Degree Service for external students working for London degrees. The College also provides seminars and tuition at its local centres. The College also designs and publishes texts and other materials for use by adults in colleges and institutions.

NICEC – National Institute for Careers Education and Counselling
Resources Centre for organisers of courses for training guidance and counselling staff, research and development work on courses, education and counselling.

NYB – National Youth Bureau
The Bureau was launched in July 1973 and absorbed the previous body, the Youth Service Information Centre. It provides a forum for association, discussion and joint action in the broad field of adolescent social education and is managed by a Council representing teachers, youth workers, social workers and others in the youth field. It offers information services including an enquiry service and a range of publications; services to training including the development of aids; and services to research. It is an independent charitable trust funded by the Department of Education and Science.

OBA
Proposed Open Broadcasting Authority — see Chapter 6

OECD — Organisation for Economic Co-operation and Development
The OECD was set up under a Convention signed in Paris on 14 December 1960, which provides that the OECD shall promote policies designed to 1. achieve the highest sustainable economic growth and employment and a rising standard of living in Member countries, while maintaining financial stability, and thus to contribute to the development of the world economy; 2. contribute to sound economic expansion in Member as well as non-member countries in the process of economic development and 3. contribute to the expansion of world trade on a multi-lateral, non-discriminatory basis in accordance with international obligations. The Members of OECD are Australia, Austria, Belgium, Canada, Denmark, Finland, France, the Federal Republic of Germany, Greece, Iceland, Ireland, Italy, Japan, Luxembourg, the Netherlands, New Zealand, Norway, Portugal, Spain, Sweden, Switzerland, Turkey, and the United States.

OU — Open University
The Open University was set up in 1969 to provide higher education by home-study methods for adults in full-time employment or working in the home. Students are generally over the age of twenty-one and do not need academic qualifications in order to apply. The University offers three forms of education — undergraduate, post-experience and postgraduate. By far the largest intake of students is at undergraduate level. The University's undergraduate teaching programme began in 1971 with 24,000 students. There are now about 65,000 students.

Schools Council
The Schools Council for the Curriculum and Examinations is an independent body with a majority of teacher members. It was established in 1964 to undertake in England and Wales research and development work in curriculum, teaching methods and examinations in schools, and to advise the Secretary of State on matters of examinations policy. The Council is financed by equal contributions from local education authorities and the Department of Education and Science.

Socio-Economic Groups[1]
AB — Managerial, administrative or professional occupation at a senior or intermediate level
C1 — Supervisory or clerical occupation ie white collar and junior managerial administrative or professional
C2 — Skilled manual worker
DE — Semi-skilled and unskilled manual workers, State pensioners and widows (widows with no other wage-earner in the household) and casual workers

1 Survey Research Practice by Hoinville G, Jowell R and Associates — Heinemann Educational Books — London 1977

STEP — Special Temporary Employment Programme (see also under MSC)
Programme set up in 1978 within the wider YOP programme to provide temporary jobs on a similar basis to those mounted under the Job Creation Programme. No project is mounted without the agreement and support of trade unions and local employers. In a full year it will provide 25,000 temporary jobs for those aged 19 and over on schemes of benefit to the community. People employed on STEP projects are paid the appropriate agreed rate for the job. The length of time which a person can be employed under STEP is limited to 12 months, although individual projects may continue for longer.

TUC — Trades Union Congress
National federation of trades unions. The TUC Education Committee is a standing committee of the TUC General Council and is responsible for TUC policy in the field of public education and also concerning the provision of educational services for trade unions and their members. The TUC has been concerned for many years about all forms of educational facilities available to workers, both for the pursuit of liberal studies and for the furtherance of social and recreational interests. The General Council is represented on the governing bodies of the Workers' Education Association, Hillcroft College and Ruskin College. TUC trade union educational services include postal courses and regional educational programmes provided with the co-operation of 140 public educational agencies comprising mainly day schools, and day-release courses.

TSD — Training Services Division/TSA — Training Services Agency
See Manpower Services Commission

UVP — Unified Vocational Preparation
A programme of coherent schemes involving the participation of the Department of Education and Science, the education authorities, the colleges, the careers services, The Training Services Division, the Industries Training Boards, and employers, depending which agencies are appropriate to a particular scheme, organised so as to assist a young person to make successful progress during the transition from school to work and adolescence to adulthood. The word 'scheme' is used rather than 'courses' because it is based upon the principle that experiences from which young people can learn take place in a variety of contexts, and that this learning can be facilitated and extended by a variety of agencies.

WEP — Work Experience Programme
An MSC programme introduced in September 1976 to provide unemployed young people aged 16–18 with an opportunity to learn about different kinds of jobs and gain systematic practical experience of a range of different trades. Facilities were provided by employers in both public and private sectors (largely in service industries) and the Education Service also ran associated courses for WEP trainees. The programme has now been superseded by the Youth Opportunities Programme (see below).

Youthaid
A research and pressure group set up in April 1977 to campaign on behalf of young people, particularly those who are neither in employment nor receiving continuing training and education.

YOP — Youth Opportunities Programme (see also under MSC)
Programme to provide work preparation courses and many different kinds of work experience for unemployed young people. The Youth Opportunities Programme is available to any young person under 19 who has been unemployed for 6 weeks or more and to all unemployed summer school leavers from September 1978 onwards. In a full year it will provide 234,000 16, 17, and 18 year olds with an opportunity of training and work experience, together with jobs for 8,000 unemployed adults as supervisors.

Local Radio Stations

BBC

Radio Birmingham	Radio London
Radio Blackburn	Radio Manchester
Radio Brighton	Radio Medway
Radio Bristol	Radio Merseyside
Radio Carlisle	Radio Newcastle
Radio Cleveland	Radio Nottingham
Radio Derby	Radio Oxford
Radio Humberside	Radio Sheffield
Radio Leeds	Radio Solent
Radio Leicester	Radio Stoke on Trent

Independent	*Area Served*
Beacon Broadcasting	Wolverhampton/Black Country
BRMB Radio	Birmingham
Capital Radio	London
Radio City	Liverpool
Radio Clyde	Glasgow
Down Town Radio	Belfast
Radio Forth	Edinburgh
Radio Hallam	Sheffield & Rotherham
LBC	London
Metro Radio	Tyne/Wear
Radio Orwell	Ipswich
Pennine Radio	Bradford
Piccadilly Radio	Manchester
Plymouth Sound	Plymouth
Swansea Sound	Swansea
Radio Tees	Teeside
Thames Valley Broadcasting	Reading
Radio Trent	Nottingham
Radio Victory	Portsmouth

Glossary

Independent Television Companies	*Area Served*
Anglia Television	East of England
ATV Network*	Midlands
Border Television	Borders and Isle of Man
Channel Television	Channel Islands
Grampian Television	North-East Scotland
Granada Television*	Lancashire
HTV	Wales and West of England
London Weekend Television*	London
Scottish Television	Central Scotland
Southern Television	South of England
Thames Television*	London
Tyne Tees Television	North-East England
Ulster Television	Northern Ireland
Westward Television	South-West England
Yorkshire Television*	Yorkshire

Independent Television News

---

* 'Major' companies with network responsibilities.

Bibliography

Ashton, D.N. and Field, D. – *Young Workers* – Hutchinson – 1976

Ball, C. – *Community Service and the Young Unemployed* – National Youth Bureau – 1977

Bazalgette, J.L. – *School Life and Work* – London Grubb Institute – 1973

BBC Audience Research Department – *A Summary of Recent Research into Cinema-going and Television Viewing* – BBC ARD Report VR/75/660 – 1975

BBC Audience Research Department – *Annual Review of BBC Research Findings* – 1977

BBC/IBA – *Using Broadcasts in Schools (The Hayter Report)* – 1974

Belson, W.A. – *The Impact of Television* – Crosby, Lockwood – 1967

Blumler, J.G. and Katz, E. (eds) – *The Uses of Mass Communications* – Sage Publishing Inc – 1974

Brannen, P. (ed) – *Entering the World of Work: Some Sociological Perspectives* – HMSO – 1975

British Youth Council – *Youth Unemployment: Causes and Cures* – Report of a Working Party – March 1977

Brown, R. – *Characteristics of Local Media Audiences* – Teakfield – 1978

Carrick James Market Research Ltd. – *A National Survey amongst 7–17 Year Olds* (for Pye Ltd., Cambridge) – 1978

Cherry, N. – *Persistent Job Changing: is it a Problem?* – Occupational Psychology – 1976

Community Relations Commission – *Unemployment and Homelessness* – a report – HMSO – 1974

Dembo, R. and McCron, R. – *Social Factors in Media Use* – in Brown, R. (see above)

Education and Science, Department of – *Careers Education in Secondary Schools* – HMSO – 1973

Education and Science, Department of – *Careers Education in Secondary Schools: Education Survey 18* – HMSO – 1973

Education and Science, Department of – *Curriculum 11–16 by HM Inspectorate* – December 1977

Education and Science, Department of – *Education in Schools: a consultative document* – HMSO Cmnd 6869 – 1977

Education and Science, Department of – *Education Statistics for the United Kingdom* – HMSO – 1975

Education and Science, Department of – *Report by HM Inspectors on curricula for non-participant 16–19s* – 1976

Education and Science, Department of – *16–19, Getting Ready for Work* – HMSO – 1976

Education and Science, Department of – Statistics of Education, Vol. 2 *School Leavers CSE and GCE* 1976–1978 Vol. 3 *Further Education* – 1976

EEC – *From Education to Working Life* – December 1976

EEC – *Youth Employment* – April 1977

Ellis, C. (compiler) – *Current British Research on Mass Media and Mass Communication* – Centre for Mass Communications Research, University of Leicester – 1977

Employment, Department of – *Unqualified, Untrained and Unemployed* – HMSO – 1970

Employment Service Agency – *The Transition from School to Work: A Critical Review of UK Research Literature* – Report No. 49 by Linda Clarke – 1978

Engineering Industry Training Board – *The Relevance of School Learning Experience to Performance in Industry* – EITB – 1977

Fogelman, K. – *Leaving the Sixth Form* – National Foundation for Educational Research

Fogelman, K. (ed) – *Britain's Sixteen Year Olds* – National Children's Bureau – 1976

Gordon, A.G. and Williams, G.L. – *Attitudes of Fifth and Sixth Formers to School, Work and Higher Education, Lancaster* – PICE – 1977

Government Statistical Service – *Government Statistics: brief guide to sources* – 1978 edition

Government Statistical Service – *Social Trends No. 8* – HMSO – 1977

Government Statistical Service – *United Kingdom in figures* – 1977 edition

Greenberg, B. – *Viewing and Listening: Parameters among British Youngsters* – in Brown, R (ed) – *Children and Television* – Collier Macmillan, London – 1976

Harris, Marjorie – *How to Get a Job* – Institute of Personnel Management – 1976

Harrison, R. – *The Demoralising Experience of Prolonged Unemployment* – Department of Employment Gazette – April 1976

Hearnden, A. – *Paths to University: Preparation, Assessment, Selection* – MacMillan Education Ltd. – 1973

Hill, J.M.M. – *The Transition from School to Work* – Tavistock Institute – 1969

Hill, J.M.M. and Scharff, D.E. – *Between Two Worlds: Aspects of the Transition from School to Work* – Richmond, Surrey – Careers Consultants Ltd. – 1976

Home Office – *Report of the Committee on the Future of Broadcasting (The Annan Report)* – Cmnd 6753–1 – August 1977

House of Commons – *Report on the Attainment of the School Leaver* – 1977

House of Commons – *Report on People and Work* – 1978

House of Commons Select Committee on Race Relations and Immigration – HMSO 1969 and 1976

IBA — *A Survey on the Relationship between Children and Television* Phase 1 — 1972

Institute of Education of the European Cultural Foundation — *Youth Education Employment* — 1977

International Publishing Corporation — *Teenage Girls: A Market Expenditure Study* — 1977

International Publishing Corporation — *The Children's Market* — 1970

Keil, E.T. — *Becoming a Worker* — Leicestershire Committee for Education and Industry/Training Services Agency — 1976

King, E.J., Moore, D.H. and Mundy, J.A. — *Post-compulsory Education: A New Analysis in Western Europe* — Sage — 1975

Kirton, M. — *Career Knowledge of Sixth Form Boys, London* — Careers and Occupational Information Centre — 1976

Law, Bill and Watts, A.C. — *Schools, Careers and Community* — research by National Institute for Careers Education and Counselling — pub. Church Information Office for the General Synod Board of Education — 1977

Lomas, G. — *The Inner City* — London Council of Social Service — 1974

Maizels, J. — *Adolescent Needs and the Transition from School to Work* — Athlone Press — 1970

Manpower Services Commission — *MSC Review and Plan, 1977*

Manpower Services Commission — *Towards a Comprehensive Manpower Policy* — 1976

Manpower Services Commission — *Young People and Work (The Holland Report)* — MSC — 1977

Manpower Services Commission *Young People and Work. Manpower Studies No. 19781* — HMSO — MSC — 1978

Manpower Services Commission/Training Services Agency — *Training for Skills* — 1977

Maxwell, J. — *Reading Progress from 8—15* — NFER Publishing Co. — 1977

McCann Erickson Advertising Ltd. — *A Survey of Youth in Britain* — 1977

McCann Erickson Advertising Ltd. — *The McCann Erickson European Youth Study* — 1979

McCann Erickson Advertising Ltd. — *You Don't Know Me* — 1977

McQuail, D. — *Sociology of Mass Communications* — Penguin Books — 1972

Moore, C.H. — *From School to Work* — London — Sage — 1976

Moore, T. — *School and the Developing Concepts of Work, Responsibility and Freedom.* Paper for International Society for the Study of Behavioural Development — 1977

Moore, T. and Clautour, S.E. — *Attitudes to Life in Children and Young Adolescents* — Scand. J. Psychol. 1977, 18 10—20.

Mukherjee, S. — *There's Work to be Done* — HMSO — 1974

Mukherjee, S. — *Job Creation and the Case for the Corner Shop* — in Personnel Management Sept. 1977

National Foundation for Educational Research in England and Wales — *Educational Provision: 16—19* by Dean and Choppin and *One Year Courses in Colleges and Sixth Forms* by Vincent and Dean.

National Foundation for Educational Research in England and Wales — *Alternatives to the Traditional Sixth Form* — to be published.

National Youth Bureau *Youth into Industry* NYB Leicester 1977

Neave, G.R. — *How they Fared: the Impact of the Comprehensive School upon the University* — Routledge & Kegan Paul — 1975

OECD — *Beyond Compulsory Schools* — 1976

OECD — *Entry of Young People into Working Life* — 1977

OECD — *Report of the Joint Working Party on Education and Working Life* — 1977

OPCS in collaboration with Prof. G. Williams and A. Gordon — *16 and 18 year olds: Attitudes to Education* — DES Report No. 86

Paul, L. — *School Leavers' Attitudes to Work and School* — Department of Psychology, Sheffield University — 1977

Rauta, I. and Hunt. A., OPCS — *Fifth Form Girls: their Hopes for the Future* — HMSO — 1975

Robins, D. and Cohen, P. — *Knuckle Sandwich* — Penguin Books — 1978

Rodmell, O.B.E. — *Economic Perspective on Youth People's Employment* — MSC — 1978

Rubber and Plastics Processing Industry Training Board — *Education Needs of 14–19 Year Olds* — RPITB — 1976

Rubber and Plastics Processing Industry Training Board — *School Curriculum for a Changing World* — RPITB — 1976

Rubber and Plastics Processing Industry Training Board — *Education and Work* (working title): 3rd Report of the RPITB Study Group — to be published.

Schools Council — *Sixth Form Survey, Vol. I (1970) Vol. II (1970) Vol. III (1971)* — London Books for Schools

Singer, E.J. and MacDonald, I.D. — *Is apprenticeship outdated?* — Institute of Personnel Management — 1970

Smith, Parker & Smith (eds) — *Leisure and Society in Britain* — Allen Lane — 1973

Sunday Times, The — *The Sunday Times Supplement to the National Readership Survey* — Jan–Dec 1977

Thomas, R.K. and Weatherall, C.D., OPCS — *Looking Forward to Work* — HMSO — 1974 (Part I of Youth Employment Study; Part II to be published)

Trades Union Congress — three mimeographed papers — 1977
The 16–18s: The Next Steps
Statement on Priorities in Continuing Education
Note of comment on the Government's consultative paper *Education in Schools*

Weir, D. and Nolan, F. — *Glad to be Out?* — Scottish Council for Research in Education — 1977

Willis, P. — *Lads, Lobes and Labour* — in *New Society* 20 May 1977

Youthaid — *Young People, Employment, Education and Training: a bibliography* — 1977

Youthaid — *The Youth Opportunities Programme: Making It Work* — 1978

Youthaid — *Youthaid Activities: a Discussion Document* — 1977